Inexpensive Science Experiments for Young Children

Grades K–1

by
Deirdre Englehart

Published by Instructional Fair
an imprint of
Frank Schaffer Publications®

Instructional Fair

Author: Deirdre Englehart
Editor: Diana Wallis
Cover Artist: Jannette Bole
Interior Designer: Jannette Bole

Frank Schaffer Publications®

Instructional Fair is an imprint of Frank Schaffer Publications.

Send all inquiries to:
Frank Schaffer Publications
3195 Wilson Drive NW
Grand Rapids, Michigan 49544

Inexpensive Science Experiments for Young Children—grades K–1

ISBN: 0-7424-2789-7

1 2 3 4 5 6 7 8 9 10 MAZ 10 09 08 07 06 05 04

Table of Contents

Published by Instructional Fair. Copyright protected.
0-7424-2789-7 *Inexpensive Science Experiments for Young Children*

🎲 Standards Correlation Chart 🎲

Category/Standard	Page(s)
Category: Science as Inquiry As a result of activities in grades K–4, all students should develop	
• abilities to do scientific inquiry	6–7, 9–10, 77
• understanding about scientific inquiry	7–10, 77
Category: Physical Science As a result of the activities in grades K–4, all students should develop an understanding of	
• properties of objects and materials	11–19
• position and motion of objects	20
Category: Science and Technology As a result of the activities in grades K–4, all students should develop	
• abilities of technological design	21, 23–24, 26–27, 29–32
• understanding about science and technology	22–25
• abilities to distinguish between natural objects and objects made by humans	22, 28
Category: Life Science As a result of the activities in grades K–4, all students should develop an understanding of	
• the characteristics of organisms	33–61
• life cycles and organisms	41, 54
Category: Earth Science As a result of activities in grades K–4, all students should develop an understanding of	
• properties of earth materials	71
• changes in earth and sky	62–71
Category: Science in Personal and Social Perspectives As a result of activities in grades K–4, all students should develop an understanding of	
• types of resources	72–76
• changes in environments	72–76

Published by Instructional Fair. Copyright protected.

0-7424-2789-7 *Inexpensive Science Experiments for Young Children*

Introduction

Your students will have so much fun with the activities in this book that they will be thrilled to discover they are learning science. The activities focus children's natural curiosity and desire to explore on pursuits that will move them toward scientific literacy—and, for some, toward becoming scientists. They will learn to propose a hypothesis, to test it, to observe what happens, and to report their results. They will be learning the scientific method, developing their thinking and reasoning abilities, and having fun playing with things like rocks and mud. What could be better than that?

As an aid to learning, you can have students create covers so they can assemble lab pages about their work into a lab book. Student lab books will be useful for review and to show parents. You can use the lab page template on page 79 for many of the activities.

The activities are based on the standards for science content in the *National Science Education Standards*. If these standards are somewhat new to you, they are available in print or online at the Web site of the publisher, the National Academy Press. The site provides not only the standards but also a full explanation of the purpose, process, and persons involved in developing them.

Here is a summary statement of the goals of the standards and of their value.

> All of us have a stake, as individuals and as a society, in scientific literacy. An understanding of science makes it possible for everyone to share in the richness and excitement of comprehending the natural world. Scientific literacy enables people to use scientific principles and processes in making personal decisions and to participate in discussions of scientific issues that affect society. A sound grounding in science strengthens many of the skills that people use every day, like solving problems creatively, thinking critically, working cooperatively in teams, using technology effectively, and valuing life-long learning. And the economic productivity of our society is tightly linked to the scientific and technological skills of our work force....
>
> The intent of the *Standards* can be expressed in a single phrase: Science standards for all students. The phrase embodies both excellence and equity. The *Standards* apply to all students, regardless of age, gender, cultural or ethnic background, disabilities, aspirations, or interest and motivation in science. Different students will achieve understanding in different ways, and different students will achieve different degrees of depth and breadth of understanding depending on interest, ability, and context. But all students can develop the knowledge and skills described in the *Standards*, even as some students go well beyond these levels.
>
> By emphasizing both excellence and equity, the *Standards* also highlight the need to give students the opportunity to learn science. Students cannot achieve high levels of performance without access to skilled professional teachers, adequate classroom time, a rich array of learning materials, accommodating work spaces, and the resources of the communities surrounding their schools. Responsibility for providing this support falls on all those involved with the science education system.
>
> —*National Science Education Standards*

A standards correlation chart (page 4) summarizes which standards each activity addresses. The book is divided by science category. At the beginning of each new category—unit—is a brief reiteration of the appropriate standards so that your higher goal in the various activities is in view.

0-7424-2789-7 *Inexpensive Science Experiments for Young Children*

As a result of activities in grades K–4, all students should develop abilities necessary to do scientific inquiry and understanding about scientific inquiry.

Secret Messages

abilities necessary to do scientific inquiry
- Ask a question about objects, organisms, and events in the environment.
- Plan and conduct a simple investigation.
- Communicate investigations and explanations.

Materials
- toothpicks, lemon juice, paper (Engage, Explore)
- milk, vinegar, lamp, or sunlight (Engage)

Engage
Use a toothpick dipped in lemon juice to write a message to your students. Allow the paper to dry before the lesson. Tell the students that you have written them a secret message. Ask volunteers to read the message.

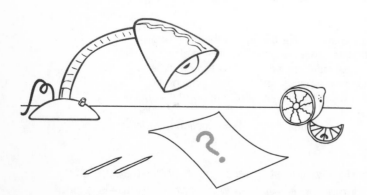

Explore
Take the paper outside in a sunny spot or move it back and forth over a light. As the paper and lemon juice warm up, students will be able to read the message.

Encourage students to test the lemon juice, vinegar, and milk by writing their own messages. They can take their messages out in the sun or hold them over a lamp. Ask them to discuss what happened and decide which secret formula made the best messages.

Develop
Discuss with students why these substances are good for writing secret messages. Students can give their ideas. Tell them that the liquids contain acids. The acids change part of the paper to sugars, and the heat makes the sugars turn brown, so you can see the secret writing.

Extend
Students can create secret messages to their families. They can take the messages home and let family members try to figure out how to read them.

Perfect Pennies

abilities necessary to do scientific inquiry
- Ask a question about objects, organisms, and events in the environment.
- Plan and conduct a simple investigation.
- Communicate investigations and explanations.

understanding about scientific inquiry
- Scientists use different kinds of investigations depending on the questions they are trying to answer. Types of investigations include describing objects, events, and organisms; classifying them; and doing a fair test (experimenting).

Materials
- pennies, soap, tooth brush to scrub with (Engage)
- Lab page (p. 79), lemon juice, vinegar, salt, ketchup, paper or plastic bowls, cotton balls, paper plates, paper towels (Explore)

Engage
Brainstorm ways to clean the pennies. Students can test some of the standard ways such as scrubbing them, using soap, etc.

Explore
Put small amounts of lemon juice, vinegar, salt, mixture of vinegar and salt, and ketchup in bowls. Write the substances on the board. Say, For this activity you will test some different solutions to see if any will clean the pennies. Write each substance on your lab page. Next to it, write if the substance cleaned a penny or did not clean it. Students will put pennies on paper plates and use cotton balls to dip into the substances and rub the pennies.

- lemon juice
- vinegar
- salt
- vinegar and salt mixed
- ketchup

Develop
Have students each flip a penny to get heads or tails. Each student then finds another person who got the same result and discusses the question with that person. Ask, What did you find out from your experiments? Which substances cleaned pennies? Which substances did not clean pennies? Why do you think some substances worked well for cleaning?

Extend
Have students try to clean other objects like spoons, other coins, keys, etc., with the same ingredients. Ask, What did you find out?

Milk Mystery

understanding about scientific inquiry
- Scientists use different kinds of investigations depending on the questions they are trying to answer. Types of investigations include describing objects, events, and organisms; classifying them; and doing a fair test (experimenting).

Materials
- glass of milk (Engage)
- lab page (p. 79), bowls, milk, food coloring, liquid detergent (Explore)

Engage
Drink a glass of milk, giving yourself a milk moustache. Give the class a big smile and ask them if they have seen an advertisement that looks like you. Ask them if they like milk.

Explore
Students can work in pairs or groups. Encourage them to use their lab pages to write or draw what happens. Remind them not to taste the experiment.

1. Have students half fill a bowl with milk.
2. Place three or four drops of different colors of food coloring evenly around the milk surface.
3. Next, on top of each drop of food coloring, add a drop of detergent. Say, Watch the colors swirl around. Record what happens on your lab page.
4. Look carefully at the edge of the bowl. What is happening? *Students will see the colors slide down the side of the bowl as well as across the milk surface.*

Develop
Discuss why the colors moved as they did. Ask, Do you know what molecules are? They are tiny particles that make up milk—and everything else. The milk molecules were dancing along together to form the surface of the milk. Food coloring joined the dance by just fitting in among the milk molecules. But along came Detergent! Detergent breaks apart the dancing molecules of milk, causing the milk to shrink away from the drops of detergent. The food coloring helps us to see what happened.

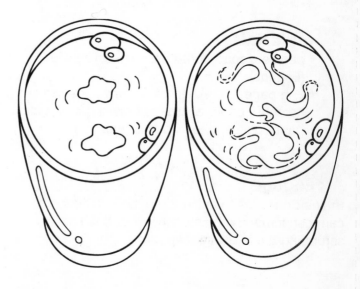

Extend
Wash your hands with soap. Soap acts like the detergent by breaking apart the molecules of dirt on your hands so you can get your hands clean.

0-7424-2789-7 *Inexpensive Science Experiments for Young Children*

Egg Extravaganza

abilities necessary to do scientific inquiry

- Ask a question about objects, organisms, and events in the environment.

understanding about scientific inquiry

- Scientists use different kinds of investigations depending on the questions they are trying to answer. Types of investigations include describing objects, events, and organisms; classifying them; and doing a fair test (experimenting).

Materials

- jar, egg, water, salt, spoon (Engage)
- heat-proof glass bottle with mouth slightly smaller than the diameter of an egg, peeled hard-cooked egg, heat source, water (Explore)

Engage

Place an egg in a jar of water. Ask students to observe the egg. Does it sink or float? *It sinks.*

Ask students if they think adding salt to the water can make the egg float. They can vote by raising their hands. Add salt to the water, one teaspoon at a time, stirring gently. Have students keep count of how many teaspoons you add. The egg will begin to float at some point.

Explore

You may wish to practice this in advance. Do this experiment as a demonstration, because it involves hot water.

1. Put a small amount of water in a bottle and heat it to boiling.

2. Remove the bottle from the heat and immediately place a peeled hard-cooked egg on the mouth of the bottle, forming a light seal.
3. As the bottle cools, the egg will drop into the bottle.

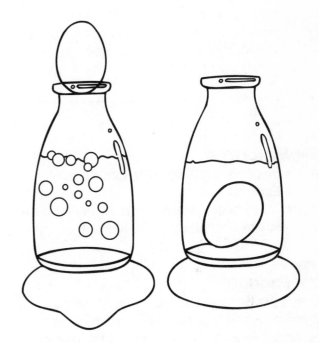

Develop

Explain that air expands when heated. The air in the bottle expanded, forcing some air out of the bottle. As the air cooled, the egg sealed the bottle so no air could get back in. The cooling air in the bottle took up less space and caused less pressure. But the air outside the bottle kept putting out just as much pressure as before. So the higher air pressure pushed the egg into bottle.

Extend

Have students act out what happened to the egg in the demonstration.

0-7424-2789-7 *Inexpensive Science Experiments for Young Children*

Bewildering Balloons

abilities necessary to do scientific inquiry
- Ask a question about objects, organisms, and events in the environment.
- Plan and conduct a simple investigation.

understanding about scientific inquiry
- Scientists use different kinds of investigations depending on the questions they are trying to answer. Types of investigations include describing objects, events, and organisms; classifying them; and doing a fair test (experimenting).

 Materials
- medium-sized round balloons (Engage, Explore)
- wooden or metal skewers longer than the inflated length of the balloons (Explore)

 Engage

Blow up a balloon and release it. Show the students that the balloon is just an ordinary balloon. Allow students to inspect the balloon to be sure it is not a trick balloon.

Explore

Ask students to predict what will happen if you push a skewer through the balloon.

Blow up the balloon again and tie the end off. Blow it up until it's firm but not too big.

Carefully push and twist a skewer through the balloon at the darker spot opposite the knot where the balloon rubber is thick. (If the balloon breaks, just start over with a new one. Scientists don't always succeed the first time.) Slide the skewer through to the knot area, pushing it through the knot. The skewer should then be completely through the balloon. A little cooking oil on the skewer may increase your rate of success.

Allow students to try the experiment themselves. (Be sure they are supervised while using the skewers.)

Develop

Explain and discuss why this amazing experiment works. Everything is made of molecules. The molecules of latex—balloon material—connect to each other in long chains. If you work the skewer in carefully at the places where the chains of molecules aren't stretched too thin, the skewer will fit between the chains.

Extend

Students can try other balloon tricks such as a balloon rocket or a balloon launcher.

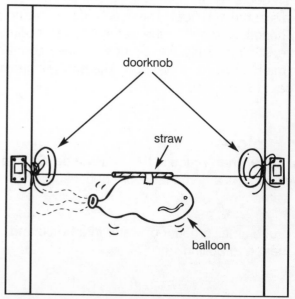

Balloon Rocket

As a result of the activities in grades K–4, all students should develop an understanding of properties of objects and materials; position and motion of objects; and light, heat, electricity, and magnets.

Is It a Solid or a Liquid?

understanding properties of objects and materials

- Materials can exist in different states—solid, liquid, and gas.

Also addresses science as inquiry standards for abilities necessary to do scientific inquiry and understanding about scientific inquiry.

Materials

- cup of juice, cookie (Engage)
- lab page (p. 79), various food items such as water, milk, juice, bread, chips, molasses, honey, sugar, etc. (Explore)
- poster-making materials (Develop)

Engage

Show students a cup filled with juice and a cookie. Ask them to tell you about the two items.

Explore

If students don't bring it up, introduce the idea that juice is a liquid and that a cookie is a solid. Have students brainstorm other objects that are liquids and solids. Record their ideas on the board.

Encourage students to sort and classify the following objects in the categories of solids or liquids: water, milk, juice, bread, chips, molasses, honey, sugar, etc. Say, Write your lists on your lab page.

Develop

Students can work in groups to develop a definition of solids and liquids. Each group can create a poster with the definition and a picture that explains what they know. Show the posters to the whole class. Decide together on definitions of solids and liquids, combining all the information from the different groups. *(Definitions should include the ideas that a liquid flows and fits the shape of the container it is in; a solid has shape and form—no matter what we put it in, the shape and size do not change.)*

Extend

Have a solid and liquid search throughout the classroom, school, or even at home. Have children record the items that are solids and liquids.

0-7424-2789-7 Inexpensive Science Experiments for Young Children

A Mysterious Substance

understanding properties of objects and materials

- Objects have many observable properties, including size, weight, shape, color, temperature, and the ability to react with other substances.
- Materials can exist in different states— solid, liquid, and gas.

Also addresses science as inquiry standards for abilities necessary to do scientific inquiry and understanding about scientific inquiry.

Materials

- *Bartholomew and the Oobleck*, bowl of oobleck (Engage)
- lab page (p. 79), large mixing bowl, measuring cups, cornstarch, water, green food coloring, spoons, paper cups, napkins (Explore)

Engage

Read the story *Bartholomew and the Oobleck* by Dr. Seuss, or tell the children that you have found a mysterious substance. Show them a bowl of oobleck.

Explore

Encourage children to help you measure and mix the oobleck.

1 cup cornstarch
1/2 cup of water at room temperature
a few drops of green food coloring
(For a large batch, use 10 cups cornstarch, 6 cups water—enough for about thirty students.)

Encourage children to explore the oobleck to get a good sense of what it is. They can hold it in their

hands, try making it into a ball, pulling it apart, etc. On their lab pages, children should record how it looks, feels, and smells.

Develop

Ask, Is oobleck a liquid or a solid? What makes you think so? The class can discuss the questions. Then divide the class in half. One half can come up with reasons why oobleck is a solid and the other half can come up with reasons why they believe oobleck is a liquid.

Extend

Allow children to mix different amounts of cornstarch and water to further explore liquids and solids. What happens when the mixture is different? Does the substance act the same way or differently?

Liquid Explorations

understanding properties of objects and materials

- Objects have many observable properties, including size, weight, shape, color, temperature, and the ability to react with other substances.
- Materials can exist in different states—solid, liquid, and gas.

Also addresses science as inquiry standards for abilities necessary to do scientific inquiry and understanding about scientific inquiry

 ## Materials

- gallon jug of water (Engage)
- lab page (p. 79), securely closed bottles labeled 1–8, enough sets for each group:
  - #1 plain water
  - #2 colored water
  - #3 corn syrup
  - #4 cooking oil
  - #5 liquid dish soap
  - #6 liquid hand soap
  - #7 fabric softener
  - #8 chocolate syrup (Explore, Extend)
- Liquid Observations chart (Develop)

 ## Engage

Show students a large jug of water and ask, Is this a solid or a liquid? What are some examples of liquids? How do they feel? How do they act? Do liquids act like solids?

Explore

The bottles should not be opened for any reason during this part of the lesson.

Give each group a set of eight bottles of liquids. Students can shake the bottles, swirl them, tip them, hold them upside down, etc. They can write down what they notice about the different liquids by writing the numbers on their science lab page, including some describing words and even a guess about what each liquid is. They can also write comments about which liquids seem similar in the ways they move.

 ## Develop

Encourage children to discuss what they observed about the liquids. On a chart labeled Liquid Observations, write words that describe the various liquids. As people give words, groups can discuss which bottles fit that description.

Extend

Encourage students to open the bottles and feel the liquids. See if they can add additional comments to describe the liquids based on what they feel.

0-7424-2789-7 *Inexpensive Science Experiments for Young Children*

Solid Liquid

understanding properties of objects and materials

- Objects have many observable properties, including size, weight, shape, color, temperature, and the ability to react with other substances.

Also addresses science as inquiry standards for abilities necessary to do scientific inquiry and understanding about scientific inquiry.

 Materials

- access to a freezer, plastic jars with lids (Explore)

 Engage

We have been learning about liquids. Can anyone think of a way to make a liquid a solid? Have students share their ideas.

 **Explore**

Give each child a plastic jar with a lid. Students can write their names on the jars or on labels affixed to the jars. Have them fill the jars to the top with water. They can then set the lids loosely on the jars without tightening them. Be sure all the containers are full to the brim when they are placed in the freezer. After a day or two, children can remove the jars and notice what has happened.

 **Develop**

Ask, What happened to the water? *It froze—became a solid.* What happened to the lids? Why? *Solid water—ice—takes up more space than liquid water.*

Extend

Make frozen juice treats. Use paper cups and craft sticks. Encourage children to predict how long the treats will take to freeze. Eat the treats after they have frozen.

0-7424-2789-7 *Inexpensive Science Experiments for Young Children*

Ice Cold

understanding properties of objects and materials

- Objects have many observable properties, including size, weight, shape, color, temperature, and the ability to react with other substances.
- Materials can exist in different states—solid, liquid, and gas.

Also addresses science as inquiry standards for abilities necessary to do scientific inquiry and understanding about scientific inquiry; earth and space science standards for properties of earth materials.

Materials

- ice cubes, salt, thread (Engage)
- lab page (p. 79), ice cubes, small pieces of towel, thin fabrics, sheets, plastic, foil (Explore)
- ice cubes with craft-stick handles, paper, finger paint or tempera (Extend)

Engage

Show how you can pick up an ice cube with a thread. Ask students why they think you are able to do this. Teach children the trick to show their families. Give each child an ice cube and a piece of thread. Each will place the thread across the top of an ice cube and sprinkle salt on it. The salt will melt the ice, then the ice will refreeze over the thread. When a student picks up the thread, it will lift the ice cube.

Explore

Explain to students that they will be testing materials to see which substances best insulate their hands from cold. Provide a large bowl of ice cubes and put pieces of fabric, stiff plastic, and aluminum foil next to it for students to try. Which materials best protect children's hands from the cold as they handle the ice cubes? They can write their results on their lab pages.

Develop

Teach children this song to the tune of "Mary Had a Little Lamb." Encourage them to tell what they discovered about the ice and materials.

Ice cubes are so cold to touch, cold to touch, cold to touch. Ice cubes are so cold to touch, they make my hands feel cold.

Ice can change into a liquid, to a liquid, to a liquid. Ice can change into a liquid, it melts back into water.

Extend

Make ice cube paintings. Give the children finger paint to put on paper. They can use their finger tips to put dots of paint around the paper. Then they can use an ice cube with a craft-stick handle to spread the paint around to create an ice cube painting.

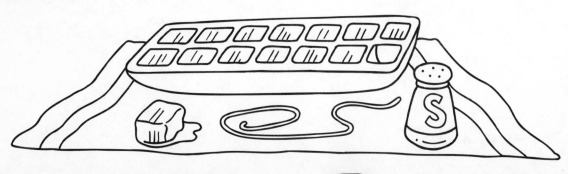

Help! I'm Melting!

understanding properties of objects and materials

- Objects have many observable properties, including size, weight, shape, color, temperature, and the ability to react with other substances.
- Materials can exist in different states— solid, liquid, and gas.

Also addresses science as inquiry standards for abilities necessary to do scientific inquiry and understanding about scientific inquiry; earth and space science standards for properties of earth materials.

Materials

- glass of ice water (Engage)
- lab page (p. 79), plastic cups of ice (Explore)

Engage

Show children a glass of water with ice cubes in it. Tell them you are really thirsty and need a cold drink. Ask them to decide how to keep the drink so the ice cubes won't melt. Encourage children to brainstorm items in the classroom they could use to help keep the drink cold.

Explore

Students can collect the classroom materials they mentioned earlier that they think will help keep the ice cubes frozen. Give each group two ice cubes. Urge them to explore what they can do to keep the ice cubes from melting. Time groups to see how long they can keep their ice cubes solid. Have students record on their lab pages what they do to keep the ice cold and how successful they are.

Develop

Teach students this rhyme.

You may think that ice is a solid today,
But out of the freezer you might be dismayed.
The ice cube will melt and no longer be
The solid that you see!

Extend

Have children do the same activity but this time they will try to melt the ice cube as fast as they can!

Where Did the Water Go?

understanding properties of objects and materials

- Objects have many observable properties, including size, weight, shape, color, temperature, and the ability to react with other substances.
- Materials can exist in different states—solid, liquid, and gas.

Also addresses science as inquiry standards for abilities necessary to do scientific inquiry and understanding about scientific inquiry; earth and space science standards for properties of earth materials.

Materials
- paint brushes, water (Engage)
- lab page (p. 79), small pie tin, ice, hot water, clear glass cup (Explore)
- mirrors (Extend)

Engage
Give children paint brushes and water to paint on the blackboard or outside on a sidewalk. Ask them to watch what happens to their paintings.

Encourage students to blow on their paintings to see if that makes them disappear even quicker. Tell them the word for what happens is *evaporation*.

Explore
Students can perform this experiment with hot tap water.

1. Put ice in a small pie tin.
2. Pour hot water into a clear glass cup.

3. Cover the cup with the pan of ice.
4. Observe.
   Evaporation is happening. Evaporation means tiny bits of water are mixing with the air to form water vapor. The water vapor moves up to the cool air. On your lab page, draw what happens. Use a magnifier to look closely.

Develop
Water on the ground will *evaporate*—it will disappear into the air and eventually end up in clouds. Air contains water vapor. Look up the word *evaporate* and create a class story about a puddle that evaporated into the clouds. Once upon a time there was a large rain puddle…

Solids to liquids and liquids to gas—
Water changes as the days and seasons pass.
As a solid it is cold and doesn't change shape,
But a liquid takes the shape of any container you make.

As a gas it evaporates, like it has gone away!
But we may see it again as rain someday.
Solids to liquids and liquids to gas
Water changes as the days and seasons pass.

Have students explain the cycle of water and how water can be changed into different states.

Extend
Breathe on mirrors. How does the cloudy place feel? Is it wet or dry? Talk about where or when you may have seen this happening at home, in the bathroom, etc.

0-7424-2789-7 *Inexpensive Science Experiments for Young Children*

Freezer Pops

understanding properties of objects and materials

- Objects have many observable properties, including size, weight, shape, color, temperature, and the ability to react with other substances.
- Materials can exist in different states— solid, liquid, and gas.

Also addresses science as inquiry standards for abilities necessary to do scientific inquiry and understanding about scientific inquiry; earth and space science standards for properties of earth materials.

 Materials

- unfrozen freezer pops (Engage)
- salt, unfrozen freezer pops, large plastic cups, ice (Explore)
- frozen freezer pop (Develop)
- lab page (p. 79), plastic cups, salt (Extend)

 **Engage**

Show students a box of thawed freezer pops. Say, I have a problem, we were supposed to have these freezer pops this afternoon for a special treat and I forgot to freeze them. Any suggestions? Discuss any possibilities students suggest.

Explore

Give each student a plastic cup of ice, an unfrozen freezer pop, and salt.

Students should stick their freezer pops in the cups of ice and pour in some salt. Have them move the cup around and lightly jiggle it up and down. Continue this process until the pop begins to freeze. Turn the pop over and try on the other end.

The pop will not completely freeze but will become slushy. Students can eat their frozen pops.

Develop

Create a Venn diagram and help students compare and contrast the frozen freezer pop with the one they froze in the experiment. *(Example of differing characteristics: slushy/hard, cold/colder, partly frozen/frozen; similarities: taste, color, etc.)*

What made the freezer pop cold? Did the whole thing freeze? Do you think it would freeze harder if you continued with the experiment?

 Extend

Students can put two cups of water in the freezer, one with a tablespoon of salt, one with no salt. They can check them at one-hour intervals to find out which one freezes quickest. They can record their data on their lab page.

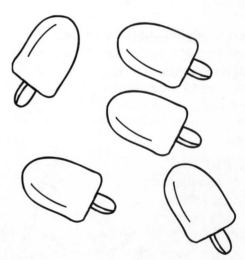

0-7424-2789-7 *Inexpensive Science Experiments for Young Children*

Invisible Gas?

understanding properties of objects and materials

- Objects have many observable properties, including size, weight, shape, color, temperature, and the ability to react with other substances.
- Materials can exist in different states—solid, liquid, and gas.

Also addresses science as inquiry standards for abilities necessary to do scientific inquiry and understanding about scientific inquiry; earth and space science standards for properties of earth materials.

Materials

- plastic cup, pan or bowl with 2–3" of water (Engage)
- for each group, lab page (p. 79), balloon, water or soda bottle, hot water, ice water (Explore)
- pictures of hot-air balloons, paper, crayons (Extend)

Engage

Students will enjoy doing this experiment themselves. Turn a cup upside down. Put it straight down into the water, then slightly tip the cup, but keep the lip of the cup underwater. Ask, What did you see? Was something in the cup? *(Students will usually see some bubbles when the cup goes into the water, then a large bubble of water when the cup is tipped, because air was in the cup.)*

Explore

Students can work in groups. Be sure a helper or parent supervises the hot water. Put a balloon over the mouth of the bottle. Explain that there is air in the bottle and it can't get out because of the balloon. Encourage students to predict what might happen when they put the bottle in hot water. Discuss. Have them try it out. Have them record what happens on their lab pages. *(After a few minutes, the balloon will begin to inflate.)*

Encourage students to predict what will happen if they put the bottle in cold water. Discuss. Encourage them to try it. Have them record their observations. *(The balloon will deflate and may even be pulled into the bottle.)* Encourage the students to experiment by moving the bottle back and forth between the pans of hot and cold water.

Develop

Discuss what the experiment shows about air. *It takes up space, when it is hot it expands, when it is cold it contracts, or shrinks.* Encourage students to draw two pictures on the lab page to show what happened.

Extend

Show students pictures of hot-air balloons. Discuss how warming the air makes the balloons rise so they can fly. Letting the air cool brings the balloon back down. Students can draw and color their own hot-air balloons.

0-7424-2789-7 *Inexpensive Science Experiments for Young Children*

Got Gravity?

Materials
- Frisbee (Engage)
- lab page (p. 79), stone, coin, other objects to test for gravity (Explore)

Engage
I have a special antigravity toy. This is a supersonic Frisbee. I can throw it up in the air and it will never come down. Raise your hand if you believe me. Ask children why they don't believe you. Throw the Frisbee. Say, Oh, no! It is broken!!

Explore
Show students a small stone in one hand and a coin in the other hand. Ask them to predict which object will hit the ground first if both are dropped from the same height. Students can write their predictions on their lab pages. Test the experiment by dropping the two objects at the same time. Ask for student comments. *Students should hear the stone and the coin hit at the same time.*

Allow children to test additional materials on their own. Provide additional rocks, balls, paper, toys, and so on.

Develop
Ask students for ideas about what gravity is. Record their ideas and then come up with a definition of gravity that includes the idea that gravity is a force that pulls on everything on earth all the time. Gravity is always pulling everything toward the center of the earth.

> Gravity, gravity pulls me down—
> I stick on the earth—I don't fly around!
> I throw a ball way up in the air—
> I won't loose my ball, it falls down right there!

Extend
Students can test drop other objects to learn if they can detect a difference in the rate the objects fall.

*Frisbee is a registered trademark of WHAM-O Inc.

0-7424-2789-7 *Inexpensive Science Experiments for Young Children*

As a result of activities in grades K–4, all students should develop abilities of technological design, understanding about science and technology, and abilities to distinguish between natural objects and objects made by humans.

Balancing

abilities of technological design

- Identify a simple problem.
- Propose a solution.
- Implement proposed solutions.

Also addresses life science standards for the characteristics of organisms and physical science standards for using simple tools.

 ## Materials

- straight-backed chair (Engage)
- lab page (p. 79), balances, collections of rocks, shells, teddy bears, and other items (Explore)
- wire, nuts, bolts (Extend)

 ## Engage

Have a student sit in a straight-backed chair, with both feet flat on the floor and hands in his or her lap. The student's back should touch the chair back. Ask the student to stand up. Then, tell the student to try again to stand, but this time without leaning his or her body forward or moving any other muscles. The student won't be able to stand without leaning forward because of balance. Encourage all the students to test this in their seats with a partner checking that they aren't leaning forward.

 ## Explore

Model using a balance scale. Encourage children to use a balance scale to balance different materials. Provide rocks, toys, shells, etc. Ask students to record the results on their science lab pages.

 ## Develop

Invite students to draw pictures of times when they need to use their own balance. Remind them to think about sports, the playground, walking, riding a bike, etc. Show the pictures and discuss balance.

Extend

Students can create toys out of wire, nuts, and weights that will balance on their fingers. They should work to create something that can balance on one finger.

Machines That Move Us

understanding about science and technology

- People have always had problems and invented tools and techniques to solve problems.

abilities to distinguish between natural objects and objects made by humans

- Some objects occur in nature; others have been designed and made by people to solve human problems and enhance the quality of life.

Also addresses physical science standards for understanding position and motion of objects.

 Develop

Have students work in pairs to mirror or mimic the movements of a partner. Encourage them to take turns being the mirror.

 Extend

Use riddles to have students identify different kinds of motion or objects that demonstrate a kind of motion. For example, I am on the playground and people go back and forth on me as they play. What am I? (*swing*) I am on the playground. Two people balance on me as they play. I go up and down. What am I? (*teeter totter*)

 Materials

- skis, skates, crutches, wheel chairs, bicycle, skateboard, snowshoes, etc. (Engage, Explore)

 Engage

Bring in a variety of objects (skis, skates, crutches, wheel chair, bicycle, skateboard, snowshoe, paddle board) that make it easier for people to move along different surfaces. Allow students to explore the items (but not use them).

Explore

After students have examined the various objects, discuss why each item makes moving easier. Students can identify one surface on which each object helps movement and one surface on which the object would make movement harder.

Levers for Lifting

abilities of technological design

- Identify a simple problem.
- Propose a solution.
- Implement proposed solutions.
- Evaluate a product or design.
- Communicate a problem, design, and solution.

understanding about science and technology

- People have always had problems and invented tools and techniques to solve problems.

Also addresses physical science standards for understanding position and motion of objects.

Materials

- brick, various tools such as screw driver, wedge, hammer, etc. (Engage)
- lab page (p. 79), books, string, ruler or yardstick, fulcrum (Explore)
- tools, including a hammer, a wedge, a screwdriver, and a scraper (Develop)
- blocks of wood with nails driven most of the way in, claw hammers (Extend)

Engage

Outside, show children a brick in the dirt. Ask, How strong are you? Challenge them to move the brick—without touching it. Provide some tools. Children can discuss ideas for how to move the brick. Encourage students to use some of the tools to try various ways to move the brick.

Explore

Ask, Which is easier, to lift this stack of books by using a loop in this string or by using this ruler as lever? Students can write their predictions on the lab page.

Have children try lifting the books with the string. How much success did they have? Have them write what happens on their lab pages.

Next, set up the ruler as a lever. Students can try lifting the books by pushing on the other end of the ruler. Have them write what happened on their lab pages. Encourage students to explore by setting the fulcrum at different positions and testing how easy or hard the books are to lift. Remind them to write on their lab pages. They can draw pictures of the lever with the fulcrum at different points.

Develop

A lever helps you do more work without using more muscle. Look at various tools such as a hammer, a wedge, a scraper, and a screw driver. Decide if any of these tools are used as levers. Explain your thinking. Take a class vote to see if there is agreement about the tools.

Extend

Provide some blocks of wood with nails driven most of the way in. Encourage students to try pulling the nails out with their fingers. Then provide claw hammers and show students how to pull out the nails. Explain how the hammer works as a lever. Encourage them to try pulling out the nails, too. (Of course, this activity must be well supervised.)

23

0-7424-2789-7 *Inexpensive Science Experiments for Young Children*

Down the Ramp

abilities of technological design

- Identify a simple problem.
- Propose a solution.
- Implement proposed solutions.
- Evaluate a product or design.
- Communicate a problem, design, and solution.

understanding about science and technology

- People have always had problems and invented tools and techniques to solve problems.

Also addresses physical science standards for understanding position and motion of objects.

Materials
- ball, board (Engage)
- assortment of balls, boards, blocks or books, rulers (Explore)
- lab page (p. 79), pencils (Develop)
- toy cars and trucks, small objects to use for weights (Extend)

Engage
Say, I want to roll this ball across the floor. What can I do to make it go farther? Allow all children to give their ideas. Then suggest rolling the ball down a board. Ask children if they think it will work. Try it out.

Explore
Have children work to roll identical balls down two different ramps. Make one ramp about four inches high and the second about eight inches high. Children will build the ramps out of boards and blocks or books. Another board can be placed about a foot from the ends of the ramps so students can see which ball is the fastest.

Place a block on the bottom of each ramp and see how far the ball will move it. Encourage the children to try the experiment other ways (with different sizes, weights of balls, different heights of ramps, etc.).

Develop
Write three sentences on your lab page telling what you found out during the experiment.

Extend
Conduct the same experiment but use cars and trucks instead of balls. After you initially see which cars go the fastest, add weights to the cars and make other changes to try to increase speed.

0-7424-2789-7 *Inexpensive Science Experiments for Young Children*

Up the Ramp

understanding about science and technology

- People have always had problems and invented tools and techniques to solve problems.

Also addresses physical science standards for understanding position and motion of objects.

Materials

- board, ball, books or blocks of wood (Engage)
- lab page (p. 79), sturdy suitcase or book bag with enough weight to make it challenging for a child to lift, smooth board (Explore)

Engage

Show students a ramp and have them predict how far a ball will go beyond the end of the ramp. Explain to them that ramps are fun for playing, but they can also come in handy when moving or lifting things.

Explore

Ask, Can you remember a time when you walked up a ramp? Do you think it was easier to go up a ramp than to climb stairs? Ramps can be useful for lifting things other than our own bodies, too.

Challenge the children to try to lift a book bag and put it on the table. Next, take a long board and lean it against the table. Have students experiment to see if it is easier to roll the book bag up the ramp. Have them record their findings on their lab pages.

Students can search for ramps on the school ground and think about how ramps help when moving things.

Develop

Why was it easier to move the book bag up the ramp instead of lifting it? What activities would be good for using a ramp instead of lifting? *(loading a truck with boxes, loading cars on a car carrier, rolling a wheelchair or a cart up a ramp rather than lifting the person or the cart up the steps, etc.)*

Extend

Students can use LEGO parts to build ramps for racing marbles or balls.

*LEGO is a registered trademark of the LEGO Group.

Rollers or Wheels?

abilities of technological design

- Identify a simple problem.
- Propose a solution.
- Implement proposed solutions.
- Evaluate a product or design.
- Communicate a problem, design, and solution.

Also addresses physical science standards for understanding position and motion of objects.

Materials

- large box (Engage)
- sturdy boxes large enough for a student to sit in, jump ropes or other ropes, broom handles or dowels, wagon or wheeled cart (Explore)

Engage

If I gave you this large box to take home to your family, how would you plan to get it home? Ask students to discuss ideas for moving the box.

Explore

Students can work in groups to compare ways to move things: dragging, using rollers, and using wheels.

1. Have one child in each group sit in a cardboard box. Help students tie a rope around the box. They can pull on the rope to move the person in the box.

2. Place the box on sturdy broom handles. (Keep the rope on the box.) Have one child sit in the box. Pull on the rope to move the person and the box. Others in the group can pick up broom handles from the back and put them in front to try to keep the box moving. (Supervision is key to keep accidents from happening with the broom handles.)

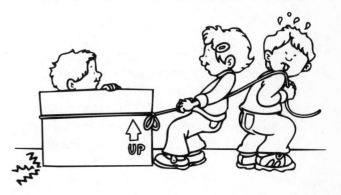

3. Place the box in a wagon. Have a child sit in the cardboard box in the wagon. Group members pull on the rope to move the person.

Develop

Discuss with students which way of moving someone was easiest and why.

Extend

Students can volunteer to use the wagon to deliver books to various classrooms or to the library. Students can create posters to advertise this service and distribute them to the office and to the teachers.

0-7424-2789-7 *Inexpensive Science Experiments for Young Children*

The Incredible Moving Machine

abilities of technological design
- Identify a simple problem.
- Propose a solution.
- Implement proposed solutions.
- Evaluate a product or design.
- Communicate a problem, design, and solution.

Materials
- shoe boxes, toilet paper rolls, paper towel rolls, cardboard, sticks, scraps of wood, rubber bands, pipe cleaners, tape, etc. (Explore)

Engage
Brainstorm machines we use in our society. Graph all the machines the students can brainstorm. As a class decide on the way to organize the graph (for example, machines that take us places, machines that help us prepare food).

Explore
Children should sketch plans for "incredible moving machines" they can build from materials on hand— shoe boxes, toilet paper rolls, cardboard, sticks, scraps of wood, rubber bands, glue, pipe cleaners, tape, etc.

Then they can build the machines they planned. You can have a class show of all the inventions, and students can explain the uses for their machines and how they work.

Develop
Students can draw advertisements for their machines. Ads should explain what each machine does and convince people that this machine will make a difference in their lives.

Extend
Children can bring in different toys that move and try to figure out how they move.

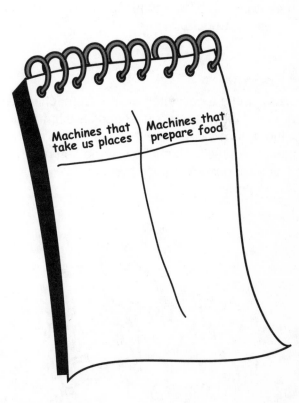

Machines that take us places | Machines that prepare food

Take It Apart!

abilities to distinguish between natural objects and objects made by humans

- Some objects occur in nature; others have been designed and made by people to solve human problems and enhance the quality of life.

Also addresses physical science standards for properties of objects and materials.

Materials

- broken machines such as clocks, toasters, typewriters, fax machines, answering machines, phones, VCRs, computer CPUs (Engage)
- tools such as wrenches, pliers, screwdrivers, wire cutters (Explore)

Engage

Show students a collection of broken machines. Ask them if they have suggestions for what to do with them. If no one suggests taking them apart, suggest it yourself. Then show some common tools and model how to use them to take something apart.

Explore

Safety precautions:
1. **Do not** take apart **TVs, computer monitors, or smoke detectors** (TVs and computer monitors can have high voltages even when unplugged; some smoke detectors use radioactive elements).
2. Do not take apart plugged-in equipment.
3. Safety goggles are a good idea.
4. Students should wash their hands when finished.

Students can work in small groups. Each group will have one or two broken machines, empty pie tins, and tools. Encourage children to use different tools to take apart the appliances. (Be sure students are well supervised, especially when using screw drivers or other sharp tools.)

Develop

Children can report on what machines they took apart, how they did it, and what they learned about the machines. Ask questions such as How did you use the tools?

Extend

Children can sort and classify the parts from the appliances. They can then create collages using the parts.

Strong Structures

abilities of technological design

- Identify a simple problem.
- Propose a solution.
- Implement proposed solutions.
- Evaluate a product or design.
- Communicate a problem, design, and solution.

Provide toothpicks and marshmallows or gum drops. Guide students in creating some basic structures.

Next, have students try different shapes and experiment to see what shapes are best for building. Students can predict what shapes will be the strongest. They can test the strength of shapes by placing toys on top of them.

Materials
- gumdrops, toothpicks, cups (Explore)

Engage
Have you ever heard a story where a house is blown down? I think it was a straw house and it must not have been very strong. (Students will be happy to retell the story to you.)

Explore
Tell students, Today it is your job to figure out what is the best shape house to build so it won't get blown down.

Develop
Each group should create a visual that shows what they found out about the various shapes and structures they created. Tell them to be sure to include what shape they found to be the strongest.

Extend
Create the highest tower or longest building with the materials.

Building Bridges

abilities of technological design

- Identify a simple problem.
- Propose a solution.
- Implement proposed solutions.
- Evaluate a product or design.
- Communicate a problem, design, and solution.

Materials

- "The Three Billy Goats Gruff" readers' theater, p. 31 (Engage)
- 3"-by-5" cards, tape, pennies (Explore)

Engage

Ask for volunteers to act out the story of the *Three Billy Goats Gruff*. Students can also practice and read the reader's theater of the same story. See page 31.

Explore

Ask the children if they can make a bridge to support the smallest billy goat? The medium billy goat? The largest billy goat? The troll?

Have students use the cards and tape to create a bridge that will support the billy goats. They can use six cards and six 2-inch pieces of tape. After they create the bridge, they can place pennies on it one at a time to see how much weight it will support.

Small billy goat	5 pennies
Medium billy goat	10 pennies
Large billy goat	15 pennies
Troll	8 pennies

Test your bridge to see if it will support more than one goat or troll at the same time.

Develop

Encourage students to discuss this in their groups: Things I learned about construction and building.

Extend

Allow children to build bridges using different materials. They can test the strength of their bridges.

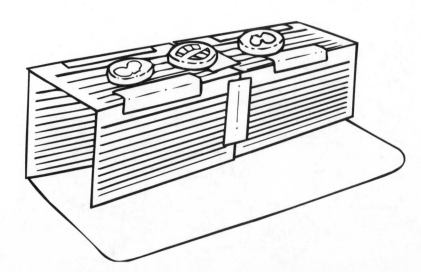

The Three Billy Goats Gruff
Readers' Theater

CAST OF CHARACTERS	
NARRATOR 1	THREE BILLY GOATS GRUFF
NARRATOR 2	TROLL

NAR. 1. Once upon a time, there were three billy goats named Gruff. The goats wanted to cross the bridge to get to the hillside to eat the green grass and make themselves fat. But a mean troll who lived under the bridge would not let anyone cross.

NAR. 2. So the three billy goats Gruff came up with a plan. The first billy goat started to cross the bridge.

ALL, *softly*. Trip trap, trip trap, trip trap

TROLL, *in his big, mean voice*. Who's that crossing my bridge?

LITTLE BGG, *in his little voice*. It is I, Billy Goat Gruff. I am going up to the hillside to make myself fat.

TROLL. No, you're not, because I'm coming up to gobble you down!

LITTLE BGG. Oh, no! Don't eat me! Eat my brother. He's coming right behind me, and he is much bigger than I am.

NAR. 2. The troll thought a bigger goat would make a better breakfast, so he let the little billy goat cross the bridge.

ALL, *a little louder*. Trip trap, trip trap, trip trap

TROLL. Who's that crossing my bridge?

MEDIUM BGG, *in his medium voice*. It is I, Billy Goat Gruff. I am going up to the hillside to make myself fat.

TROLL. No, you're not, because I'm coming up to gobble you down!

MEDIUM BGG. Oh, no! Don't eat me! Eat my brother. He's coming right behind me, and he is much bigger than I am.

NAR. 2. The troll thought the biggest goat would make the best breakfast, so he let the medium billy goat cross the bridge.

ALL, *louder*. Trip trap, trip trap, trip trap

TROLL. Who's that crossing my bridge?

BIG BBG, *in his big voice*. It is I, Billy Goat Gruff. I am going up to the hillside to make myself fat.

TROLL. No, you're not, because I'm coming up to gobble you down!

NAR. 1. With that, the troll leaped up on the bridge.

BIG BBG. Well, come right along. I have two big horns and a mean attitude, and I'll crush you to bits, body, and bones!

NAR. 2. That is what the big billy goat said—and that is what the big billy goat did.

ALL, *softly*. Trip trap, trip trap, trip trap

NAR. 1. So the last Billy Goat Gruff crossed the bridge and headed up to the hillside to make himself fat. The three goats are probably still there to this very day—and anyone can cross the bridge any time he or she wants to.

ALL. So snip, snap, snout! This tale is told out!

Huff and Puff Houses

abilities of technological design

- Identify a simple problem.
- Propose a solution.
- Implement proposed solutions.
- Evaluate a product or design.
- Communicate a problem, design, and solution.

Also addresses life science standards for understanding characteristics of organisms.

 ## Materials

- a wolf puppet or wolf ears and nose (Engage)
- lab page (p. 79), 3"-by-5" cards, tape, craft sticks, paper plates, straws, toothpicks, gum drops, tape, blow dryer (Explore)

 ## Engage

Use a wolf puppet or put on wolf ears and nose and recite the following phrase: "Little Pig, Little Pig, let me come in! Or I'll huff and I'll puff, and I'll blow your house in." Discuss the wolf in the story of *The Three Little Pigs*. Let children come to the front of the room and act out the wolf and the pigs. Take a poll on who believes a real wolf could blow down a real house.

 ## Explore

Students can work in groups to design houses. Say, Work with your group to think of a strong design for your house. Draw your design on your science lab page.

Next, build your house with the materials we have. The house may not be taped to the table.

Then, the Big Bad Blow Dryer will come around and blow on your house. (*Put the dryer on low first and then on high.*)

So, he huffed and he puffed and he _____ (*blew the house down or didn't blow the house down*).

Say, If your house was blown down, redesign it.

Develop

Create a pamphlet that tells about buildings and how to make them strong. Include information you have learned about structures.

Extend

Research information about wolves.

Play Fact or Fiction Wolves. One student at a time tells or acts out a true wolf fact or something from stories about wolves. The class tries to guess if the student was telling something true or something false. Teach the following chant for students to recite as each is selected to report a characteristic.

> *Wolfie, Wolfie is it true?*
> *The storybook tells me all about you.*
> *What is true and what is not?*
> *I think I better learn a lot!*

0-7424-2789-7 *Inexpensive Science Experiments for Young Children*

As a result of activities in grades K–4, all students should develop understanding of the characteristics of organisms, life cycles of organisms, and organisms and environments.

No One Like Me!

the characteristics of organisms

- Each plant or animal has different structures that serve different functions in growth, survival, and reproduction. For example, humans have distinct body structures for walking, holding, seeing, and talking.

Also addresses science as inquiry standards for understanding about scientific inquiry.

 Materials

- butcher paper cut in large sheets, mirrors, scissors, crayons, markers, yarn, fabric, construction paper, sequins, etc. (Explore)

 Engage

Play the attributes game with the children. You will name a physical attribute and all the children with that attribute will stand up.

I am a boy   I like to smile
I am missing teeth   I have brown eyes
I have curly hair   I have dark skin
I have two ears   I have freckles
I have blue eyes   I have straight hair
I am a girl   I have ten toes
I have a pet

As you go through the attributes, talk about how all people have some things that are the same, but each person is different and special.

 Explore

Students work with partners to trace one another's body outline on butcher paper. Have them do your outline as well. (Save it and theirs to use in a future lesson.) Students can decorate their outlines. They can add faces, hair, etc., to show how they look and their special features. Provide mirrors for children to use when looking at their faces.

Sing this song to the tune of "Frére Jacques."

There's only one me, only one me.
None the same. None the same.
I am very special, I am very special.
Yes, I am! Yes, I am!

Develop

Have each student sit with a partner and compare how the two are the same and how they are different. They can create a Venn diagram to show their similarities and differences.

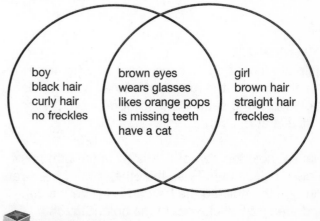

Extend

Graph the eye color, hair color, etc., of students.

Lungs Help Me Breathe

the characteristics of organisms

- Each plant or animal has different structures that serve different functions in growth, survival, and reproduction. For example, humans have distinct body structures for walking, holding, seeing, and talking.

Also addresses science as inquiry standards for abilities necessary to do scientific inquiry and understanding about scientific inquiry.

 Materials

- string, scissors (Engage)
- lab page (p. 79), plastic straws, small balloons, rubber bands, clear plastic cup with a hole in the bottom, plastic wrap (Explore)
- cotton balls, masking tape

 Engage

Say, Notice your chest as you breathe in and out. It expands and gets smaller as the air enters and leaves. Give each child a piece of string. Students can predict how big their chests are as they breathe in air by cutting the string to the size they think. Have them check to see if they are right.

Explore

Help students do this experiment in pairs. Insert a plastic straw in the mouth of a small balloon. Use a rubber band to secure the balloon and to prevent air leaks at the connection.

Make a hole the size of the straw in the bottom of a clear plastic cup. Push the other end of the straw through the hole so the balloon is inside the cup and the straw sticks out of the hole. Stretch a piece of plastic wrap over the open end of the cup. Secure the plastic wrap with a rubber band.

One partner at a time holds the cup and pulls on the "diaphragm." The other places a hand above the end of the straw sticking out of the cup. Pull down on the plastic wrap, which represents the human diaphragm, and release it. What do you feel? *(air being drawn in through the straw)* Then push up gently on the plastic wrap. What do you feel? *(air coming out of the straw)*

Draw a picture of your model. The balloon is like your lungs, and the plastic wrap is like your *diaphragm*. Your diaphragm is a muscle that separates your chest from your abdomen.

 **Develop**

Teach the students the following song to the tune of "Hokey Pokey."

I breathe the air right in.
I breathe the air right in.
I breathe the air right in
and it goes into my lungs.
I feel my chest expanding as my lungs take in the air.
Respiration is what it's called.

Ask, What happens when you breathe in air? What did you notice with our lung model? *(lungs expand, making the chest expand)*

 Extend

Students can test how strong their lungs are by blowing a cotton ball across the floor. Put a piece of tape on the floor for the starting point. Students can mark how far they could blow with another piece of tape with their name on it.

0-7424-2789-7 *Inexpensive Science Experiments for Young Children*

The Heart of Things

the characteristics of organisms

- Each plant or animal has different structures that serve different functions in growth, survival, and reproduction. For example, humans have distinct body structures for walking, holding, seeing, and talking.

 Materials

- for each stethoscope: 2 small kitchen funnels (available cheaply at dollar stores), an 18" piece of rubber tubing to fit the narrow ends of the funnels—take a funnel to a hardware store to get the right fit (Explore)

Engage

Hold up your fist. Say, There is an organ in your body that is about the size of your fist. Can you guess what it is? Give additional clues as necessary: This organ beats, it pumps all the time, and so on.

Explore

Children can make stethoscopes. They can fit the ends of a piece of tubing over the narrow ends of the funnels. You can tape the tubing in place if it isn't an exact fit. They can put one funnel on their own chests and the other funnel to an ear. Each can listen to her or his own heart and to each other's. Direct them to move the stethoscope around until they can hear the heartbeat.

Next, show them where they can feel their pulse on their necks. Say, Your pulse is caused when your heart squeezes to pump the blood through your body.

Now have children run in place for about thirty seconds. Say, Now listen to your heart again. What do you notice?

Note: Keep stethoscopes to use for the lesson on the digestive system (p. 36).

Develop

Teach students the following song to the tune of "Row, Row, Row Your Boat."

Thump, thump, thump my heart.
My heart beats all the time.
It pumps the blood to my body
and keeps me feeling fine.

Thump, thump, thump my heart.
My heart beats faster still
When I run and jump and play
instead of standing still.

Extend

After the lesson on the digestive system (p. 36), encourage students to take their stethoscopes home and use them on their families. They can report back to the class with any interesting findings.

0-7424-2789-7 *Inexpensive Science Experiments for Young Children*

Digestion

the characteristics of organisms

- Each plant or animal has different structures that serve different functions in growth, survival, and reproduction. For example, humans have distinct body structures for walking, holding, seeing, and talking.

 Materials

- stethoscopes from the activity on p. 35 (Engage)
- for each student: 2 crackers, zipper bag, small cup with water (Explore)

Engage

Have students use their stethoscopes to listen to their own and to each other's stomachs. Discuss with them what they hear.

Explore

Give each child 2 crackers, a plastic zipper bag, and a small amount of water. Children can pretend that the plastic bags are, first, their mouths, then their stomachs. Model the instructions as you give them. Say, Put the crackers in your "mouth." Close your mouth and chew up your crackers. (Students mash up the crackers in the sealed bag. They can push down on them and break them apart.) Now you swallow your food and it goes down to your stomach. Once your food is in your stomach, fluids enter to break down the food more so it will give the body what it needs. Add a small bit of water to the bag. Seal the bag again and continue to mash up the crackers. Add more water if necessary. Children should work to have only crumbs in the water.

Develop

Review with children the parts of the body that help in digestion. Encourage children to tell what they know about digestion. Read books that provide more information for students.

Extend

Experiment with different food items to see if they all digest the same. If you use meat you can add cola to the bag instead of water. The cola will simulate the acids in your stomach that help to break down food.

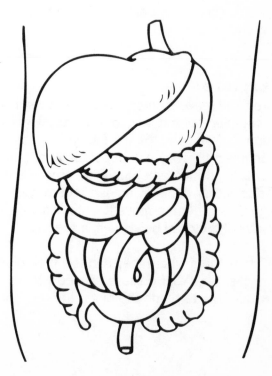

Bones Hold Me Up

the characteristics of organisms

- Each plant or animal has different structures that serve different functions in growth, survival, and reproduction. For example, humans have distinct body structures for walking, holding, seeing, and talking.

Materials

- bone cards, p. 38 (Engage, Extend)
- cleaned chicken or other bones, pieces of yarn, string, or fishing line with one end knotted, rigatoni noodles (Explore)

Engage

Pass around copies of the bone cards (p. 38). Discuss with students where their bones are in their bodies.

Explore

Give students a few minutes to find out where they have bones in their body. Have them tell some bones they discovered. Tell them that the human body contains 206 bones. Bones and muscles work together to hold up your body and help you move.

Bones don't bend—that's why we break them sometimes. So how can we bend our backs? We can bend because our backs contain many small bones connected together. These bones are called *vertebrae*.

Children can create a backbone model using string or fishing line. Tie off or tape one end so the noodles don't slide off. Students can then add the pasta vertebrae. Tie off the ends of the string as shown.

Ask children to move their backs different ways and to move the models the same ways.

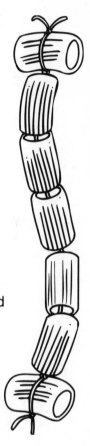

Develop

Discuss these questions with students. Why do we need bones? Can bones bend? How do we bend our bodies?

Extend

Encourage students to read books about the different bones in their bodies.

After they learn names of some common bones, they can play a bone-touching version of Simon Says. One person uses the bone cards or looks at the resource book on bones and calls out a bone—Simon says, touch your femur. Students try to guess which is the correct bone and touch it, etc.

 0-7424-2789-7 Inexpensive Science Experiments for Young Children

Bone Cards

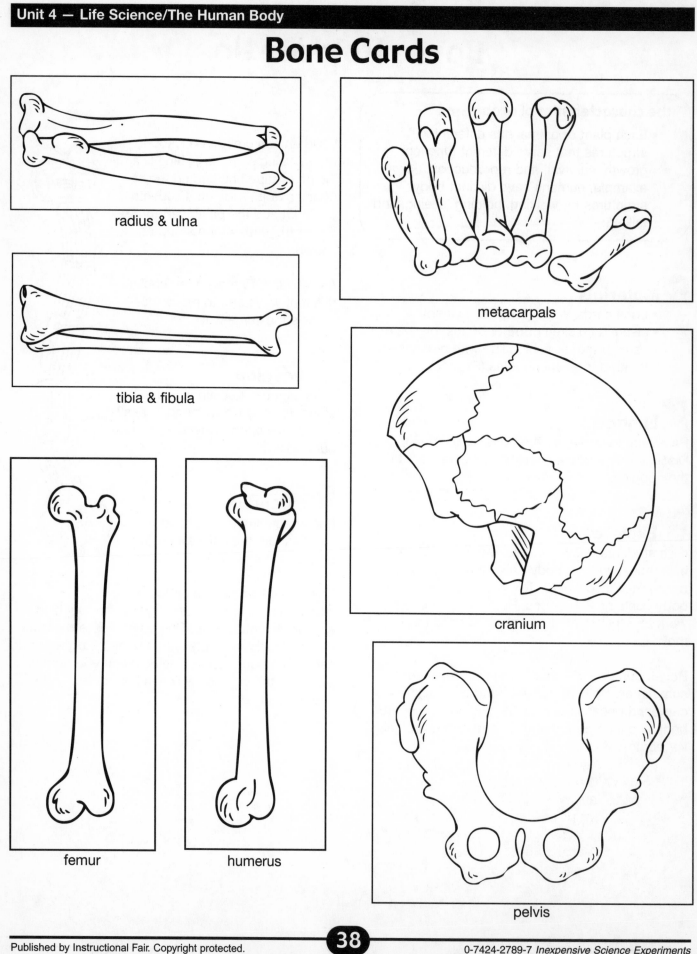

radius & ulna

metacarpals

tibia & fibula

cranium

femur

humerus

pelvis

0-7424-2789-7 *Inexpensive Science Experiments for Young Children*

Body Parts

the characteristics of organisms

- Each plant or animal has different structures that serve different functions in growth, survival, and reproduction. For example, humans have distinct body structures for walking, holding, seeing, and talking.

 Materials

- body parts page (p. 40), body cutout (see p. 33), scissors, glue (Explore)
- 3" x 5" index cards, pencils (Extend)

Engage

Play a version of Hokey Pokey. Sing the following version of the song and have students chime in with the body parts. They will enjoy the unusual gyrations required.

You put your tummy in,
You put your tummy out,
You put your tummy in
and you shake it all about.
You do the Hokey Pokey
and you turn yourself about.
That's what it's all about.

You put your backbone in....
You put your heart in....
You put your teeth right in... etc.

 Explore

Review what students know about their bodies. Talk specifically about digestion and about their hearts, lungs, and bones. Show the cutout of you. Add the different parts approximately where they belong. Students can work with their body cutouts (see p. 33). They can cut out the body parts on page 40 and glue them on their cutouts in the correct places. Encourage children to draw on additional bones, muscles, and other parts.

 Develop

Students can walk around to show classmates one thing each knows about his or her body using the body cutout.

Extend

Students can use linking cubes to measure body parts on their cutouts. They can write on 3" x 5" cards. My smile is _____ cubes. My heart is _____ cubes. My leg is _____cubes.

0-7424-2789-7 *Inexpensive Science Experiments for Young Children*

Body Parts

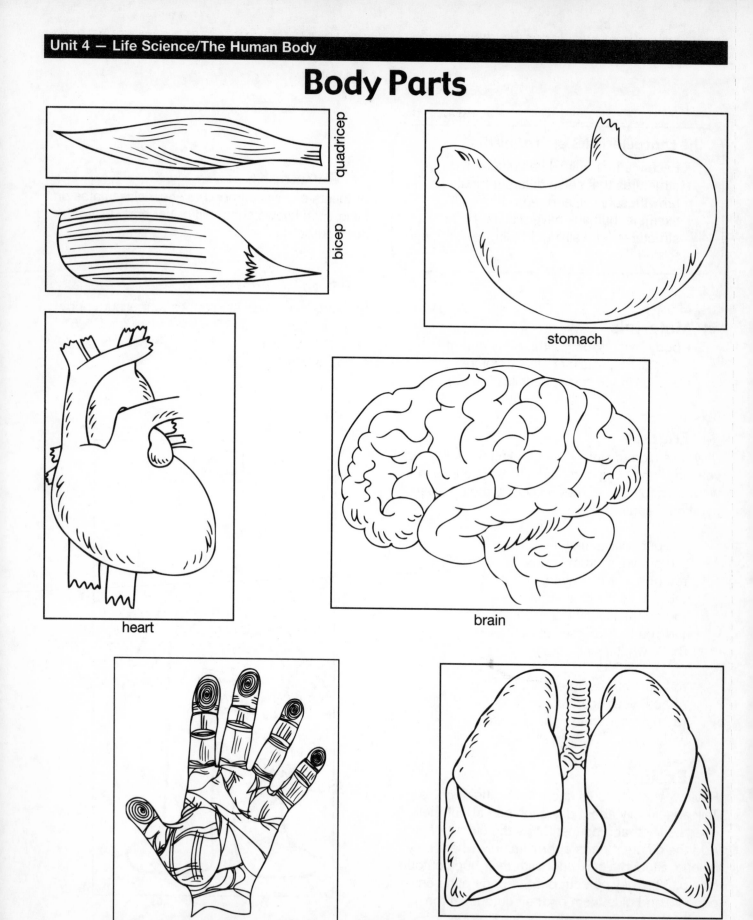

quadricep

bicep

stomach

heart

brain

skin

lungs

Growing and Changing Me

the characteristics of organisms

- Each plant or animal has different structures that serve different functions in growth, survival, and reproduction. For example, humans have distinct body structures for walking, holding, seeing, and talking.

life cycles of organisms

- Plants and animals have life cycles that include being born, developing into adults, reproducing, and eventually dying.

Materials

- baby picture of you (Engage)
- clean foam meat trays—one per student, plaster of paris, water, craft sticks, hypoallergenic hand lotion (Explore)

Engage

Show the children a picture of you as a baby. Encourage them to tell how you are the same and how you are different.

Explore

At the beginning of the school year, help students make imprints of their hands in plaster of paris. (Near the end of school, students can make second imprints and compare the two. Have you grown?) Mix plaster of paris with water. Spread it in foam trays. Have students put lotion on their hands and make a handprint in the mixture. Allow the imprints to dry. You can also measure students' heights and weights and mark them on a wall chart to compare with later measurements.

Develop

Help students create Venn diagrams that compare what they were like when they were babies to what they are like now. They can talk with their friends about the changes they have gone through and things they are able to do now that they couldn't do when they were babies.

Extend

Have students draw self-portraits of how they look today—but dressed like they will be as adults when they have careers. They can also include backgrounds to show where they will be working. Ask them to discuss or to write about what they will be doing as adults and what their jobs will be about.

0-7424-2789-7 Inexpensive Science Experiments for Young Children

My Sense of Touch

 the characteristics of organisms

• Each plant or animal has different structures that serve different functions in growth, survival, and reproduction. For example, humans have distinct body structures for walking, holding, seeing, and talking.

Also addresses science as inquiry standards for abilities necessary to do scientific inquiry and understanding about scientific inquiry.

 Materials

• pattern blocks, large brown paper bags, sticky tack, sentence strips (Explore)

Engage

Ask, What can you find out from touching things? Encourage children to talk about things they touch and how the sense of touch helps them.

Pass around different pattern blocks. Ask children to close their eyes and feel a pattern block. Ask, Can you guess what shape it is? They can look after they guess. How did you do? Were some shapes easier to identify?

Explore

Use sticky tack to attach pattern blocks to sentence strips. Create patterns with the pattern blocks and put each strip in a grocery bag. Children reach in a bag to feel the mystery pattern. They then recreate the pattern using pattern blocks or drawing it, based on their sense of touch. They can look at what is in the bag after they make their copies. Create a number of mystery patterns so students have the opportunity to try a few.

Develop

Have students create a touch poem about one thing they touch, in the following format.

Doggy,
Fluffy, soft
Furry, warm, cuddly
Doggy.

Extend

Encourage children to create their own mystery bag patterns using sentence strips, sticky tack, and pattern blocks. They can work in pairs to try to recreate each other's patterns from touch.

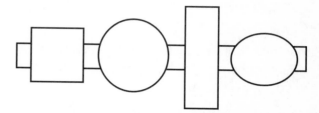

pattern strip the
student duplicates

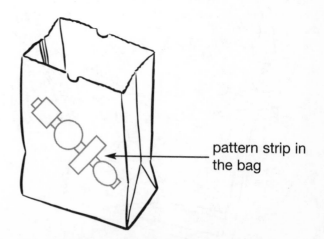

pattern strip in
the bag

0-7424-2789-7 *Inexpensive Science Experiments for Young Children*

I Make Sounds with My Body

the characteristics of organisms

- Each plant or animal has different structures that serve different functions in growth, survival, and reproduction. For example, humans have distinct body structures for walking, holding, seeing, and talking.

Also addresses science as inquiry standards for abilities necessary to do scientific inquiry and understanding about scientific inquiry.

 ## Materials

- paper, pencils, crayons, keys, pencil sharpener, paper, stapler, balloon, glass, water, ball, etc. (Engage)

 ## Engage

Do this where the children can't see you, or have a helper make the sounds out of the children's sight. Make sounds with five common items. For example, rattle keys; blow up and pop a balloon; pour water into a glass; wad up, tear, or staple papers; bounce a ball; sharpen a pencil. Ask students to identify the sounds. They can draw pictures or write words to tell each sound you create. Ask, Which things were hard to figure out? Which things were easy?

Explore

Draw a large On button or switch on the board. Students will pretend they are parts of a candy-making machine. Have them stand in a circle. Each child will play a different part of the machine and make her or his own sound and motion when the teacher presses the On button. First go one at a time around the circle, then all together. Students will enjoy stopping and starting instantly when you switch them on and off.

Develop

Encourage students to experiment making sounds with their bodies. Start with mouth sounds that don't include voices. Suggest they use lips, teeth, and tongues. What sounds can they make using their hands on their mouths? Ask, Can you change the sounds by puffing up your cheeks? How is the sound different? What sounds can you make with other parts of your body?

Extend

Students have discovered many sounds they can make with their bodies. Ask them to try to make the sounds higher or lower. They can make long sounds, short sounds, sounds that stop and start, quiet and loud sounds. Ask if sounds can show feelings. Can they make happy sounds, sad sounds, quiet sounds, loud sounds?

43

Tick Tock

the characteristics of organisms
- Each plant or animal has different structures that serve different functions in growth, survival, and reproduction. For example, humans have distinct body structures for walking, holding, seeing, and talking.

 Extend

Have students play the find the clock game at home with their parents. They can use what they have learned about how the sound travels through different items to make the game easy or hard.

 **Materials**
- windup alarm clock with a loud tick (Engage, Explore)
- newspaper, straw, popcorn, towel or other cloth (Explore)

Engage

Hide an alarm clock in the classroom, set to go off in five minutes. Challenge the children to find the clock before the alarm goes off by listening for the ticking.

Explore

Put the alarm clock in a box with different materials. Test some materials to see how much sound they allow to travel through. Some materials to test are: newspaper, straw, popcorn, towel, cloth, and so on.

Develop

Encourage students to help you create new versions of Hickory Dickory Dock.

Hickory dickory dock,
The ant crawled up the clock.
The clock struck 8,
The ant said, "Great!"
Hickory dickory dock!

My Sense of Sight

the characteristics of organisms

- Each plant or animal has different structures that serve different functions in growth, survival, and reproduction. For example, humans have distinct body structures for walking, holding, seeing, and talking.

Also addresses science as inquiry standards for abilities necessary to do scientific inquiry.

Materials

- different eyeglasses; borrow old ones from parents and families, or a local optometrist may be willing to provide them for you; try to find ones for nearsightedness, farsightedness, and astigmatism (Engage, Explore)
- simple diagram of eye (Develop)
- optical illusions (Extend)

Engage

Give students different pairs of glasses to pass around. Say, Be careful not to break or scratch the glasses. People who wear them need them to see well, so take care of them. Hold out each pair of glasses. Look at the view and look at a book. Discuss what you can see and what you can read. (Students who wear glasses should keep theirs on.) Look at the lenses of the glasses, too. Look at several different pairs.

Explore

Our eyes have to work perfectly for us to have perfect sight. The lenses in glasses help the lenses in the eyes when the eyes aren't quite perfect. Different eyeglasses fix different problems.

Eyeglasses work by bending light beams so they meet right at the *retina* in the back of our eyeballs. The retina changes light into signals that go to our brains.

Nearsightedness

Look at the eyeglasses more. Try to pick out the glasses people would use who are nearsighted. These lenses will make the view look smaller. When people are nearsighted they can see near. They cannot see clearly when things are far away. Their eyeballs may be too long.

Farsightedness

Find the glasses for people who are farsighted. These lenses will make the view look bigger or even upside down. When people are farsighted, they can see at a distance but they cannot see things clearly that are close up. One cause of farsightedness is eyeballs that are too short.

Astigmatism

Glasses for people with astigmatism change the shape of the view, stretching it out and maybe twisting it. People with astigmatism (ah-STIG-ma-tism) have a *cornea* that is out of shape. The stretched-out lens fixes it.

Develop

Show students simple diagrams of the eye with the lens, cornea, muscles, and retina labeled. Point out the different parts and encourage students to draw their own versions.

Extend

Give students optical illusions to examine.

0-7424-2789-7 *Inexpensive Science Experiments for Young Children*

My Sense of Smell

the characteristics of organisms

- Each plant or animal has different structures that serve different functions in growth, survival, and reproduction. For example, humans have distinct body structures for walking, holding, seeing, and talking.

Also addresses science as inquiry standards for abilities necessary to do scientific inquiry.

 ## Materials

- popcorn—Do this activity when you have a break from the children so you can pop the popcorn fresh and hide it in the classroom (Engage, Explore)
- magazines, scissors, paper, glue, construction paper (Develop)
- freshly popped popcorn in a zipper bag (Extend)

 ## Engage

As children return to the classroom, ask them, "What is your favorite smell?" After they discuss their thoughts, tell them you have hidden something they can smell in the classroom. Ask them how they will go about finding what you have hidden.

 ## Explore

Have the children use their noses to find the popcorn. Allow children to enjoy the popcorn when they find it.

 ## Develop

Have students cut out pictures from magazines that show people using the five senses. They can glue the pictures on construction paper.

Next, have students complete frame sentences: "I see _____ with my eyes, I hear _____ with my ears," etc.

 ## Extend

Put some freshly popped popcorn in a sealed zipper bag. Have children try to locate it. Are they able to? Discuss with them why or why not.

Taste Testers

the characteristics of organisms

- Each plant or animal has different structures that serve different functions in growth, survival, and reproduction. For example, humans have distinct body structures for walking, holding, seeing, and talking.

Also addresses science as inquiry standards for abilities necessary to do scientific inquiry and understanding about scientific inquiry.

 Materials

- paper, crayons (Engage)
- lab page (p. 79), jelly beans, lemon, bitter chocolate, pretzels—labeled sweet, sour, bitter, and salty
- chocolate bar pieces, lemonade (Extend)

 Engage

Ask students to draw pictures of foods they like. Show the pictures and talk about the favorite foods.

 Explore

Show some different food items to the students. Tell students that they will be trying foods that have very different and noticeable tastes. Ask them to taste each food and record their reaction on the lab page by making a happy face if they like it or a sad face if they don't like it.

 Develop

Say, Human beings can taste four types of taste: sweet, sour, salty, and bitter. Which food tasted salty? Which was sweet? Etc.
Which food did you like the best?
My favorite food is _____. I think this food is _____ (pick one of the four types we explored.)

 Extend

Make lemonade with the students and allow them to taste a piece of chocolate candy. Explain that these foods are made from lemons and from bitter chocolate like you tasted before, but they have been changed. Do you like these foods better now or the way they were before? What main ingredient was added to change the taste of the food items?

0-7424-2789-7 *Inexpensive Science Experiments for Young Children*

Five-Senses Scavenger Hunt

the characteristics of organisms

- Each plant or animal has different structures that serve different functions in growth, survival, and reproduction. For example, humans have distinct body structures for walking, holding, seeing, and talking.

Also addresses science as inquiry standards for abilities necessary to do scientific inquiry and understanding about scientific inquiry.

Take students on a sensory scavenger hunt either in the classroom or outside. If this is an inside activity, you might add a variety of objects not normally found in the room.

Inside

Find something that is orange.
Find something that is bright.
Find something sweet.
Find a wrapper from a food item.
Find something that makes noise.

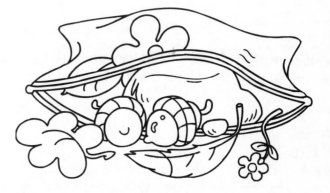

Outside

Find something in nature that makes noise. Draw a picture showing it in its environment.
Find something with a rough texture.
Find something that has a smooth texture.
Find something with an odor.

Find two other things by using your senses.

1.
2. _____

Examine all the objects collected. Do some fit more than one category? Is there an object that tastes sweet and also has a rough texture or something with an odor that is also orange?

48

0-7424-2789-7 *Inexpensive Science Experiments for Young Children*

As a result of activities in grades K–4, all students should develop understanding of the characteristics of organisms, life cycles of organisms, and organisms and environments.

All Kinds of Plants

characteristics of organisms

- Organisms have basic needs. For example, animals need air, water, and food; plants require air, water, nutrients, and light. Organisms can survive only in environments in which their needs can be met.
- Each plant or animal has different structures that serve different functions in growth, survival, and reproduction.

Also addresses science as inquiry standards for understanding about scientific inquiry.

 ## Materials

- lab page (p. 79), several varieties of young plants (Explore)

 ## Engage

I am thinking of something. I will give you clues. Try to guess what I am thinking about. It is a living thing. It grows. Sometimes it is green. *After each clue, give students time to guess that you are thinking about plants.*

 ## Explore

Bring in a variety of plants including flowering, nonflowering, and vegetable plants. Encourage children to make observations and to sort the plants according to different characteristics.

Each student chooses a plant to observe closely. Encourage students to gather information about the sizes of their plants, about the leaves, etc.

Have them draw and label their plants on a lab page, including what they think each part does.

Chart the growth of the plants over a three-week period.

Develop

Discuss with students how they sorted the plants. Ask, What features did you consider when you sorted them?

Extend

Brainstorm with the class to list possible uses for each plant. For example: trees—firewood, hold up hammock, play in, shade, lumber for houses, medicine, protection from wind. Plants used for medicine and healing can also be included.

0-7424-2789-7 *Inexpensive Science Experiments for Young Children*

What Plants Need

characteristics of organisms

- Organisms have basic needs. For example, animals need air, water, and food; plants require air, water, nutrients, and light. Organisms can survive only in environments in which their needs can be met.
- Each plant or animal has different structures that serve different functions in growth, survival, and reproduction.

Also addresses science as inquiry standards for abilities necessary to do scientific inquiry and understanding about scientific inquiry.

 Materials

- a few beans (Engage)
- lab page (p. 79), bean seeds, pots, soil, water (Explore)
- flat pieces of wood, cardboard, newspaper, string or twine, plants (Extend)

 Engage

Say, In the story *Jack and the Beanstalk*, Jack's mom just threw the magic beans out the window and they grew. If I throw these beans out the window, will they grow? Predict what you think will happen. *Throw the beans out and check on them over a five-day period.*

Explore

We will plant seeds in five pots. We will treat the pots differently to learn what plants need. For example, for Pot 1, give the plant sun, soil, and air, but no water. Number the pots.

1. No water
2. No sun
3. No soil
4. No air
5. Water, sun, soil, and air

Draw a chart to record the progress of each pot. Write what happens on your lab page.

 Develop

Discuss what you learned in the experiment—What do seeds need to grow?

Extend

Students press plants to create a herbarium. For each press, use two flat pieces of wood (such as plywood), with pieces of cardboard and newspaper sandwiched in between. Have students clip the cuttings, open the press, and place the cuttings in the middle of folded newspapers. They should include a piece of paper with the name of the plant, too, so they won't forget.

Then close the press and secure it tightly with the twine or stack heavy books or boxes on it. Store it in a warm, dry place for three or four weeks.

When someone remembers them, students can open the presses and glue the plants to construction paper. Use a mixture of 50% white glue and 50% water. Gently put the cuttings in the glue, being careful not to break them or use too much glue. Gently place the plant on a piece of construction paper. Wipe off excess glue with a tissue. Students can glue their labels on, too. When all the pieces are arranged on a page, cover them with a piece of waxed paper, sandwich them between two pieces of cardboard, and stack heavy books or boxes on top. Let the pages dry a day or two, then display them in the classroom.

0-7424-2789-7 *Inexpensive Science Experiments for Young Children*

Reaching for the Sun

characteristics of organisms

- Organisms have basic needs. For example, animals need air, water, and food; plants require air, water, nutrients, and light.
- Each plant or animal has different structures that serve different functions in growth, survival, and reproduction.

Also addresses science as inquiry standards for abilities necessary to do scientific inquiry and understanding about scientific inquiry.

Materials

- plant, window (Engage)
- lab page (p. 79), fast-growing plants, boxes, cardboard, scissors (Explore)

Engage

Place a plant next to a window for three days. Point out to students how the plant stem and leaves grow toward the light.

Explore

Use a cardboard box with a lid and strips of cardboard to create a maze, something like the one pictured, using tape or glue. Cut an opening off-center in one end of the box. If students work in groups, the holes in different boxes can be different sizes to test if the amount of light makes a difference in how much the plants grow. Place identical plants in each box. Mark the height of the plant on the edge of the box. Label the mark "Day 1." Close the open side of the box.

Draw a picture of your maze on your lab sheet showing the plant when you placed it in the maze. Open the box briefly every day to water the plant and to see where it is growing. Show on your drawing what is happening with the leaves. Label what you add to your drawing each day: Day 1, Day 2, etc.

Develop

Discuss the things that plants need. This experiment is about one thing that plants need.

Sun, sun, sun, here I come.

Designate one part of the room as the sun and ask students to travel to it as the plant did.

Extend

Students can create a story of a plant trying to reach the sun. The story can explain how a plant might have felt in the experiment—if plants had feelings.

Stems Help Plants

characteristics of organisms
- Each plant or animal has different structures that serve different functions in growth, survival, and reproduction.

Materials
- carnations, food coloring (Engage, Explore)
- lab page (p. 79), clear containers of water (Explore)

Engage

Tint several carnations by putting them in water with different colors of food coloring. Show the children the flowers and ask them to explain what they think is the reason the carnations are all different colors.

Explore

Give each student or group a carnation in water. Help the students drop food coloring into the water. Encourage students to talk about what happens and to write about it on their lab pages. Then they can make observations over time, each time noting any changes they see.

After two hours, ask, Has the flower changed? Write what has happened on your lab page.

After one day, ask, How has the flower changed? Write what has happened on your lab page.

Develop

Decide to whom you will give your flower. Write a note telling the person why you are giving her or him a flower. Tell in your note what you did to color the flower. Deliver the flowers and notes.

Extend

Conduct a stem search on the school grounds. Look for different stems and talk about the difference between stems on plants and on trees. Do bark rubbings.

0-7424-2789-7 *Inexpensive Science Experiments for Young Children*

How Do Roots Help Plants?

characteristics of organisms

- Organisms have basic needs. For example, animals need air, water, and food; plants require air, water, nutrients, and light.
- Each plant or animal has different structures that serve different functions in growth, survival, and reproduction.

Also addresses science as inquiry standards for abilities necessary to do scientific inquiry.

Materials

- plants with roots intact (Engage, Explore)
- lab page (p. 79), a large jar for each plant (Explore)

Engage

Show the students a plant with its roots. Ask them to tell you about the different parts of the plant. Point out the roots and ask students to tell you what they think the roots do for the plant.

Explore

Help students place various plants in jars with water. Mark the water level when you start. Monitor the plants and mark the water levels daily. Have students record what happens on a lab page. Help students measure the growth of the plant and of the roots.

Develop

One of the purposes of roots is to take water and nutrients to the plant and leaves. Roots also hold the plant in place.

Students can act out the process of plants growing. They can work in groups to be a plant. They can start all bunched up together and then one or two students gradually go down as the roots and others grow up as the stem and leaves. Have students move outward as the plant grows.

Extend

Have students investigate the above-ground root structures of trees around the school grounds.

Published by Instructional Fair. Copyright protected.

0-7424-2789-7 *Inexpensive Science Experiments for Young Children*

Sweet Potato Plants

characteristics of organisms

- Each plant or animal has different structures that serve different functions in growth, survival, and reproduction.

life cycles of organisms

- Plants and animals have life cycles that include being born, developing into adults, reproducing, and eventually dying. The details of this life cycle are different for different organisms.

Also addresses science as inquiry standards for abilities necessary to do scientific inquiry.

 Materials

- sweet potato, lively music (Engage)
- for each group: sweet potato, jar, toothpicks, nonchlorinated water (Explore)

 Engage

Play Hot Potato with a sweet potato. The children sit in a circle and pass the potato around as music plays. Stop the music and see who is holding the potato. That person can then control the music for the next round.

 Explore

Students can work in groups. Instruct them, Place a sweet potato in a jar, suspending it from the rim with toothpicks about a third of the way down. Fill the jar with water and put it in a warm dark place until buds and roots begin to grow. *(This will take ten to fifteen days.)* Then place the jar in a sunny window. Keep the jar in moderate sun.

Students can predict how long it will take for buds and roots to begin growing. Then they can track their daily observations on a science lab page.

 Develop

What do plants need to grow? Children can read books or use the Internet to research why some plants can grow without seeds. They can report what they learn to the class.

 Extend

Try to grow plants from branches and cuttings. Experiment to see which plants grow this way and which ones do not.

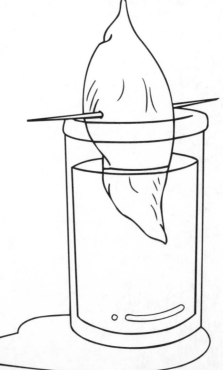

Have You Eaten Your Plants Today?

characteristics of organisms

- Each plant or animal has different structures that serve different functions in growth, survival, and reproduction.

Also addresses science as inquiry standards for abilities necessary to do scientific inquiry.

Materials

- seed, root, stem, and leaf foods such as lettuce, peanuts, asparagus, carrots, beets, broccoli, beans, corn; pieces of yarn about 18" long (Explore)

Engage

Hold up a leaf. Ask, Has anyone eaten a leaf today? Take a poll of the students.

Explore

Write on the board: roots, leaves, stems, seeds. Ask, Did you ever stop to think that we actually eat roots, leaves, stems, and seeds from plants? Give each student group two pieces of yarn to divide their table in four areas. Give each group at least one or two of each kind of food. Say, Work together to sort the foods into four groups—roots, leaves, stems, and seeds. See if everyone in your group can agree.

Develop

Review the plant parts together and have students decide if they sorted the items correctly.

Extend

Enlist parents' cooperation in students investigating the produce section of the grocery store. Have them look for the plant parts being sold and write down names of some of each. Count how many kinds of leaves are for sale. How many stems, roots, and seeds are for sale?

Discuss two other plant parts we eat—fruits and flowers. (Cauliflower and broccoli are the flowers of those plants. Any seed, or seed-containing structure, is classified as a fruit—including tomatoes and cucumbers.)

0-7424-2789-7 *Inexpensive Science Experiments for Young Children*

Animal Attributes

characteristics of organisms

- Each plant or animal has different structures that serve different functions in growth, survival, and reproduction.

Also addresses science as inquiry standards for abilities necessary to do scientific inquiry.

Materials

- animal pictures, magazines such as *National Geographic*, *Outdoors*, *Field and Stream*, etc., scissors, glue (Explore)

Engage

Write on the board as children list as many different animals as possible. Encourage children to choose from pictures of animals. Without telling the animal, they can demonstrate how it moves. The class can try to guess the animal.

Explore

1. Collect pictures of animals. Students can identify the animals in the pictures. Then attach a card identifying the animal to each picture. Students can sort the animals into groups according to categories they choose. *(To get them started, suggest size, color, how it moves, what part of the world it lives in, etc.)*

2. Divide students into small groups. Give groups magazines with a lot of animal pictures— (*National Geographic, Outdoors, Field and Stream,* etc.). Students cut out pictures of animals they find.

Each group sorts its pile of pictures into categories. Students in each group should agree on the different categories.

After groups have categorized their pictures, bring the entire class back together and let one person from each group explain why they grouped their pictures as they did. Students usually sort in interesting ways including by color, size, shape, extinct or not, eating habits, living habits, sizes of ears and tails, etc.

Develop

Create riddles about animals. Divide a sheet of paper into thirds. Write a riddle on the bottom third of the page. Create a picture of the animal in the third above the riddle, and fold the top third over it and seal it with a reusable sticker so students can look at the answer after they try to guess the riddle.

Extend

Play a sorting game. Each person selects one animal at a time and places it in the right category: insects and spiders, worms, mollusks, and vertebrates.

56

A Tree Habitat

characteristics of organisms

- Each plant or animal has different structures that serve different functions in growth, survival, and reproduction.

Also addresses science as inquiry standards for abilities necessary to do scientific inquiry.

Materials

- lab page (p. 79), a tree or other area on the school grounds suitable for viewing insects and small animals (Explore)

Engage

Where do you live? Draw a picture and tell me about your home. Say, What things do you have in your home that you need to live?

Explore

Take students to a habitat on the school grounds. A tree is a great place to find evidence of living things and life. Observe the tree. Give students the following guides for observation. They can write or draw what they see on the lab page.

Animals I saw
Possible animal homes I saw
Possible food sources for animals
Other evidence that animals have been here
Direct or indirect sources of water

Develop

Discuss, Do you know what animals would live in this habitat? What do they need to live? What animals that you didn't see do you think live here? Why do you think they live here?

Do a bark rubbing of the tree. Create a web with the tree at the center to show how it is a habitat for many animals. Discuss how the animals survive in this tree environment.

Extend

Say, Look in your own backyard, neighborhood, and park for different habitats and signs of life. Report back to the class about what you see.

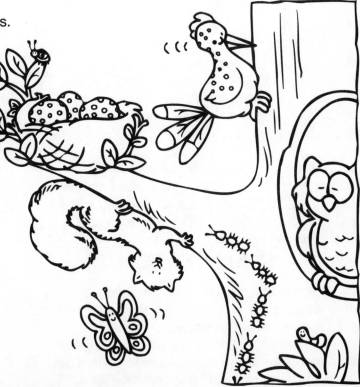

Earthworm Observations

characteristics of organisms

- Each plant or animal has different structures that serve different functions in growth, survival, and reproduction.

Also addresses science as inquiry standards for abilities necessary to do scientific inquiry and understanding about scientific inquiry.

 ## Materials

- jar of dirt (Engage)
- lab page (p. 79), a good spot for digging earthworms, jars, soil, sand, dead leaves and grass, water, plates or pans, paper towels (Explore)

 ## Engage

Show students a jar of dirt. Ask them to guess what lives in the soil.

 ## Explore

Help children dig for earthworms. Collect worms and place them in jars with layered sand and soil, with some dead grass and leaves. Add enough water to moisten the soil but do not make it wet. Observe the jars over a few days.

Put a worm on a moist paper towel and watch how it moves. How can you tell the front end from the back end? *(When it moves, the leading end is the front.)* Roll the worm over and see what happens. That is a way to tell which side is the top of the earthworm. *(The worm will right itself.)*

Think of questions you have regarding the earthworms. Design an experiment to answer one of your questions. For example, does an earthworm have the sense of touch? You could put a dry paper towel and a moist paper towel in a pan and put the worm with one end on each. Then watch to see if the earthworm prefers one or the other. You can try it several times to see if the earthworm always does the same thing. Write about it on a lab page.

When the study is complete, return the worms to the place you found them.

 ## Develop

Create a poster to tell your question and what you found out about earthworms. Report the experiment and findings to the class.

 ## Extend

Encourage students to collect other insects or small animals to observe. Warn them to check with a parent or teacher first, because some animals and insects are dangerous.

0-7424-2789-7 *Inexpensive Science Experiments for Young Children*

Bird Study

characteristics of organisms

- Organisms have basic needs. For example, animals need air, water, and food.
- Each plant or animal has different structures that serve different functions in growth, survival, and reproduction.

Also addresses science as inquiry standards for abilities necessary to do scientific inquiry and understanding about scientific inquiry.

Materials

- bird call (Engage)
- lab page (p. 79), bird feeder visible from the classroom, sticks, weeds, grass, mud, etc., paper plates (Explore)

Engage

If you have a bird call available, use it and ask the children to tell what they think it was. You can also imitate birds yourself by listening carefully and learning the sounds they make. After you have demonstrated your bird call, talk with the children about the different sounds birds make and what kinds of birds they see often.

Explore

1. Assign students to observe birds on the school grounds or in the neighborhood. They can write about what they see on a lab page.
2. Try building a bird's nest with students. Look in books or observe an actual nest. Don't take a nest from a tree unless you are sure it is not in use. Students can describe on a lab page how they build their bird's nest and how it compares to a real birds nest.
3. Students can plan, design, and build bird feeders and place them for observation during the winter. Use a bird book to identify the types of birds you see. As a class, keep a list of the different kinds of birds that visit the

feeder, with the date they are first observed. Once a bird feeder is started, it is important to continue to use it. Some birds begin to depend on it as a food source.

Develop

Write and illustrate sentence pyramids to share what you observed about birds.

I saw a bird.
I saw a blue bird.
I saw a flying blue bird.

Extend

Invite a parent of volunteer to bring parrots to the class. Observe these birds and compare them to the birds you saw outside the classroom.

0-7424-2789-7 *Inexpensive Science Experiments for Young Children*

Fur and Feathers, Skin and Scales

characteristics of organisms

- Each plant or animal has different structures that serve different functions in growth, survival, and reproduction.

Also addresses science as inquiry standards for abilities necessary to do scientific inquiry and understanding about scientific inquiry.

Materials

- fish scales, feathers, fur, animal skin, magnifiers (Explore)

Engage

Animals, Animals everywhere!
They live in the ground, the trees, and the air.
Animals need things to survive—
Food, water, and shelter, to stay alive.

What is your favorite wild animal? Discuss.

Explore

Find fish scales at a local fish market, grocery store, etc. Obtain feathers, fur, and skin from a local taxidermist. Say, Let's look at different kinds of animal coverings close up. Use your magnifiers to look at these different things, and then choose one to draw. Draw a picture of what the covering looks like magnified.

Discuss how the coverings are alike and how they are different. What are the purposes of coverings? Create a chart as a class to show your findings on the different animal coverings.

Develop

Invent an animal. Decide what to call it, what type of covering it will need, where it will live, what it will eat, etc. Draw a picture and write about your new animal.

Show your animal creations.

Extend

Students can work together to pick a specific animal that has each of the coverings listed. Each group will then create a mural that represents the habitat of that animal. Display the murals in the classroom or hallways.

0-7424-2789-7 *Inexpensive Science Experiments for Young Children*

Animals in Hiding

characteristics of organisms

- Each plant or animal has different structures that serve different functions in growth, survival, and reproduction.

Also addresses science as inquiry standards for abilities necessary to do scientific inquiry and understanding about scientific inquiry.

 ## Materials

- fabric samples in natural colors—including camouflage—and bright and bold colors

 ## Engage

Ask students if they like to play hide and seek. Ask, When you hide, how can you tell if you are in a good spot? Ask them if they think animals can play hide and seek.

Explore

Pass out various fabric samples. Students can sort them by natural and bright colors. Then half the children can take the bright-colored samples out on the playground or field area and hide them. The second half of the class will go out and search for the fabric.

Switch teams and allow the second group to hide the natural-colored fabric and the first group to hunt for those pieces.

 ## Develop

Encourage students to discuss what fabrics were easy to find and which ones were difficult to find. Ask the students to work in groups to list animals that may blend in and animals that stand out. Create a class list. Discuss why some animals try to hide and why some stick out. *(Reasons should include the ideas that the ability to blend in protects some from predators, and blending in helps some sneak up on their prey.)*

 ## Extend

Children can create pictures with hidden animals in them. They should include animals that blend in with their environments.

0-7424-2789-7 *Inexpensive Science Experiments for Young Children*

As a result of their activities in grades K–4, all students should develop an understanding of properties of earth materials and changes in earth and sky.

Weather Map

understanding changes in earth and sky

- Weather changes from day to day and over the seasons. Weather can be described by measurable quantities, such as temperature, wind direction and speed, and precipitation.

Also addresses science as inquiry standards for abilities necessary to do scientific inquiry and understanding about scientific inquiry.

Materials

- weather symbols poster (p. 63), local area map—laminate for reuse, eraseable markers (Explore)

Engage

Red sky at night, sailor's delight.
Red sky at morning, sailors take warning.

Halo around the sun or moon—
rain or snow soon.

Rainbow in the morning
gives you fair warning.

Teach these weather proverbs to students. Ask them to explain what they mean. Poll students to see if they believe these proverbs are true.

Explore

Display the word *meteorology* and the weather symbols poster (p. 63). Explain that meteorology is the study of weather. Discuss what the symbols mean. Meteorologists use symbols to put a lot of information in a small space quickly. Use a large laminated map of your local area. Children can use the symbols to show a daily weather report. Most are simple enough for them to draw, or they can cut out the symbols and tape them to the map.

Develop

Each student can create a mock weather map to exchange with a partner. The partner then makes a weather report based on the information on the map she or he is given. The partners then discuss to come to an agreement about the forecast.

Extend

Contact a local TV station to request a meteorologist to visit your school or classroom.

Help students find more information in books or online about weather topics such as severe weather. The focus can be on severe weather seen in your region or on weather in a region you are studying for social studies.

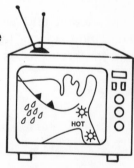

Standard Weather Symbols

Weather Event	Intensity		
	Light	Moderate	Heavy
Rain	● ●	⋮●●	●●●●
Snow	✱ ✱	✱✱✱	✱✱✱✱
Drizzle	,,	,,,	,,,
Rain shower	● ▽	● ▽	
Snow shower	✱ ▽	✱ ▽	
Freezing rain	⌒●⌣	⌒●●⌣	

Severe Weather Symbols

Thunderstorm	↗	Severe thunderstorm	↯
Drifting or blowing snow	┼→	Thunderstorm with hail	⌂↯
Hurricane	⌇	Dust storm	S→

0-7424-2789-7 *Inexpensive Science Experiments for Young Children*

Weather Watch

understanding changes in earth and sky

- Weather changes from day to day and over the seasons. Weather can be described by measurable quantities, such as temperature, wind direction and speed, and precipitation.

Also addresses science as inquiry standards for abilities necessary to do scientific inquiry.

Materials

- teddy bear, bear-sized clothing items for different seasons—cap, hat, sunglasses, mittens, scarf, jacket, bathing suit, etc. (Engage)
- outdoor thermometer (Explore)
- water colors, brushes, paper (Develop)

Engage

Bring in a teddy bear and various items to use on the bear that will show how the bear should dress in the weather. Introduce the bear to the students, show them the various items, and ask them to select the items the bear should wear on today.

Explore

1. Students can take turns playing weather reporter for two weeks. The reporter will give the temperature and a weather report each day. (Is it sunny? How much rain or snow?) Graph the results over time.

2. Students can work in groups to record the daily high and low temperatures and precipitation in one city or place for a month and graph the data for display.

Develop

Say, Create a watercolor painting of your favorite kind of weather. Write a sentence about what you do in that weather.

Extend

Students can interview family members who live in other states or countries about their weather and report what they learned to the class. Or they can do Internet research on weather in places you are studying in social studies class.

Make a Thermometer

understanding changes in earth and sky

- Weather changes from day to day and over the seasons. Weather can be described by measurable quantities, such as temperature, wind direction and speed, and precipitation.

Also addresses science and technology standards for abilities of technological design and understanding about science and technology.

Materials

- lab page (p. 79), thermometers, small clear soft drink or water bottles, food coloring, clear plastic straws, modeling clay, different colors of waterproof markers (Explore)

Engage

If I told you it is 100 degrees outside, what would you wear today? If I told you it is 60 degrees, what would you wear? If I told you it is 20 degrees, what would you wear? Explain your answers.

Explore

Help students make bottle thermometers. Fill a small soft drink bottle about 4/5 full of room-temperature water. Add food coloring. Put a clear straw in the bottle so the straw goes into the water but doesn't touch the bottom of the bottle. Seal the top of the bottle around the straw with modeling clay. Mark on the straw where the water level is. Draw the experiment on your lab page.

Move the thermometer to a sunny place. Leave it there for an hour. Does the water level in the straw change? Mark the new water level on the straw. (If time is limited, you can stand the bottle thermometer in a cup of hot tap water, then move it to a cup of cold water so students can see the movement.)

Develop

Does your thermometer work as well as a real thermometer? Explain why or why not. What kind of information do thermometers provide?

Extend

Calibrate the thermometer by comparing it to a real thermometer and marking the numbers on a new straw.

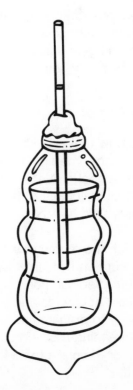

0-7424-2789-7 *Inexpensive Science Experiments for Young Children*

Find a Hot Spot

understanding changes in earth and sky

• Weather changes from day to day and over the seasons. Weather can be described by measurable quantities, such as temperature, wind direction and speed, and precipitation.

Also addresses science and technology standards for abilities of technological design and understanding about science and technology.

Materials

• graham crackers, marshmallows, chocolate bars, aluminum foil (Engage)
• lab page (p. 79), outdoor thermometers (Explore)

Engage

Show students a graham cracker with marshmallows and a chocolate bar on top. Ask them to think of the best place outside to melt s'mores. Write their suggestions on the board.

Explore

Teach students how to read a thermometer. Assist them in placing thermometers in five or six locations on the school grounds, such as under a tree, on the school building, up the flag pole, on a ledge, on the slide, etc.

Say, Predict which thermometer will have the highest temperature and which will have the lowest. Write your prediction on your lab page. Help students take hourly readings at each location until you are ready to prepare the s'mores. Graph the temperature readings. Based on the results, choose a place for the class to melt the s'mores. Enjoy your treat!

Develop

Discuss the temperature data gathered. Is there a pattern to the variations in temperature in the different places? What might one infer from the data? What could one predict from the data? The activity could be repeated several times throughout the year to provide an opportunity for students to consider energy issues related to weather.

Extend

Do this experiment at different times of the year. See if the variation in temperature at the different locations is the same or different. Consider different factors as to why the weather changes.

0-7424-2789-7 *Inexpensive Science Experiments for Young Children*

Wind Advisory

understanding changes in earth and sky

- Weather changes from day to day and over the seasons. Weather can be described by measurable quantities, such as temperature, wind direction and speed, and precipitation.

Also addresses science as inquiry standards for abilities necessary to do scientific inquiry and understanding about scientific inquiry.

Materials

- large sheets of construction paper, markers, crayons, stapler, hole punch, yarn, glue, tissue or crepe paper (Extend)

Engage

A breezy day is ideal for this lesson. Encourage students to look out windows and discuss what they can tell about the weather. If they don't mention the wind, point out moving trees, flags, etc. Tell them that wind is moving air.

Explore

Each day for two weeks, take children out to observe how the wind is moving things. (They can use their wind socks, see Extend, or their weather vanes, see p. 68.) Record observations daily. Create a graph to record information about the wind using the following scale.

Force 0	calm; leaves don't move
Force 2	light breeze; leaves rustle
Force 4	moderate breeze; small branches move
Force 6	strong breeze; large branches sway
Force 9	gale; branches break off trees
Force 11	storm; widespread damage to trees
Force 12	hurricane; severe and extensive damage

Develop

1. Over the two-week period, encourage children to tell about their weather and wind observations. They can also tell about previous experiences with wind, such as sailing a boat, flying a kite, being evacuated for a hurricane, etc.
2. Ask them to be trees and show what calm looks like. Pick different wind levels from the scale for students to demonstrate.

Extend

Children can make their own wind socks. Each child can decorate a large sheet of construction paper using markers and crayons. Then help them fold in  one long edge of the paper about an inch, which will be the top of the windsock.

Show them how to bend the paper into a cylinder shape and help them staple or glue the ends together. Use a hole punch to make three evenly spaced holes around the folded top edge.

Tie a fifteen-inch piece of yarn to each hole and tie the ends of the yarn together at the top. Students can glue tissue- or crepe-paper streamers to the bottom of the wind sock.

0-7424-2789-7 *Inexpensive Science Experiments for Young Children*

Wind Direction

understanding changes in earth and sky

- Weather changes from day to day and over the seasons. Weather can be described by measurable quantities, such as temperature, wind direction and speed, and precipitation.

Also addresses science and technology standards for understanding about science and technology.

Materials

- straws, scissors, index cards, arrowhead and tail patterns, glue, straight pins, pencils, compass (Explore)

Engage

Take students outdoors on a breezy day. Discuss ways they can detect which direction the wind is blowing. Suggest they close their eyes and face into the wind until they feel that the wind is blowing the same against each side of the face and the sound of the wind is the same in each ear. Does everyone agree on the direction the wind is coming from? They can try wetting a finger and holding it up. Ask children to look around for other clues about wind direction. (*flag, windsock, or weather vane on a building, trees, things blowing along the ground, etc.*)

Explore

Students will make simple weather vanes. Say, a weather vane tells which direction the wind is coming from. Weather vanes are usually shaped like arrows. The arrowhead always points into the wind—that is, in the direction the wind is coming from.

Make an arrow by cutting a slit in each end of a straw. Cut the arrowhead and tail shapes from index cards. Slide the arrowhead and tail into the slits and glue in place. Stick a straight pin through the middle of the straw into the eraser on the end of a pencil. The straw should swing freely. Use a marker to write compass directions around the outside of a yogurt cup—N, S, E, W. Put a lump of clay in the cup and put the pencil tip in the clay. Weight the cup with a few small stones.

Take the weather vane outside and put it on a flat surface. Show students how to use a compass to find north. Tell them to turn the cup so the N on it faces north. Ask, According to the marks on the cup, what direction is the arrow pointing? That is the direction the wind is coming from.

Develop

Ask students to think of times it might be important to know the direction the wind is blowing. (*when flying planes, when sailing boats or ships, when pitching a baseball, when forecasting weather, when launching a kite, etc.*)

Extend

Students can write poems about wind or draw pictures showing wind in action.

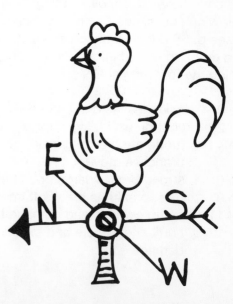

Making and Measuring Rain

understanding changes in earth and sky

- Weather changes from day to day and over the seasons. Weather can be described by measurable quantities, such as temperature, wind direction and speed, and precipitation.

Also addresses science and technology standards for abilities of technological design and understanding about science and technology.

2. Help students make a rain gauge to measure the amount of rainfall. Put a ruler in a jar and tape it at the top to hold it in place. Bend a wire coat hanger to make a holder for the jar, with the hook at the top to hang the jar over a fence or other object to give it strong support. Or use a strong rubber band to attach the rain gauge to a stick or post. Place the stick in an open area to collect the rain.

Materials

- lab page (p. 79), hot water, medicine dropper, rubbing alcohol, ice, rulers, tape, straight-sided jars, coat hangers (Explore)

Engage

Create a class sign-in with the question, "Do you like rain?" Have students sign yes or no. Sing "Rain, Rain, Go Away" with the students. Have students change the song if they like rain: Rain, rain, you're here to stay. I like the rain on this very day. Encourage students to discuss ideas about what they do on rainy days and what they do on sunny days.

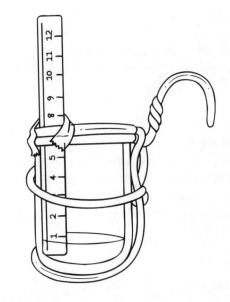

Explore

1. Do this as teacher demonstration because of the hot water and rubbing alcohol. Fill a bottle about a third full of very hot water. Add three drops of rubbing alcohol. Place a large piece of ice over the top of the bottle. Watch the rain clouds develop. When cold air bumps into warm air, tiny droplets of water are formed. This is a cloud. Encourage students to record their observations of the cloud on a lab page.

Develop

Students can sketch the cloud cover each day for a three-week period. Have them record the amount of rainfall over the same three-week period. Correlate the type of clouds to the amount of rainfall.

Extend

Create rain pictures. Use water-soluble markers to make large sections of color on a poster board. On a rainy day, put the paper out in the rain for a short time. Try the same experiment in different types of rains—soft drizzle, downpour, etc.

0-7424-2789-7 *Inexpensive Science Experiments for Young Children*

Decomposition

understanding changes in earth and sky
- The surface of the earth changes. Some changes are due to slow processes.

Also addresses life science standards for understanding organisms and environments; science in personal and social perspectives standards for understanding changes in environments.

Materials
- orange rind, lettuce leaf, foam packing peanut, bottle top, hand shovel, craft sticks, permanent marker, map of the school grounds (Explore)

Engage
Ask children to tell you what they know about buried treasure. Explain that today we will bury treasure. Children can help you create a map of the school grounds and decide on places to bury the "treasures."

Explore
Children should bury the following items on the school grounds: piece of orange rind, lettuce leaf, foam packing peanut, bottle top. Label a craft stick for each item and stick it in to mark the spot. Students can water each spot daily.

After three weeks, dig up the items that were buried. Have children discuss any changes to the materials. Discuss with them the implications of trash.

Develop
Display the word *decompose*. Have the students talk about what items decomposed and what items did not. Show students items from nature including food and other items made by people and have them predict which ones will decompose and which will not. Ask them to explain their thinking.

Extend
Have the students collect litter or sort through trash to put it into groups. What items will decompose? What items will not?

Does putting water on the soil help the items to decompose faster? Students can develop an experiment to answer that question.

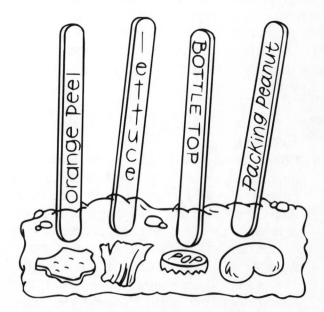

0-7424-2789-7 *Inexpensive Science Experiments for Young Children*

Water Changes the Earth

properties of earth materials

- Earth materials are solid rocks and soils, water, and the gases of the atmosphere. Earth materials provide many of the resources that humans use.

understanding changes in earth and sky

- The surface of the earth changes. Some changes are due to slow processes such as erosion and weathering, and some changes are due to rapid processes, such as landslides, volcanic eruptions, and earthquakes.

Also addresses science as inquiry standards for abilities necessary to do scientific inquiry and understanding about scientific inquiry.

Materials

- picture of Grand Canyon (Engage)
- lab page (p. 79), sand, soil, rocks, spray bottle of water, craft sticks, plastic toys (Explore)

Engage

Show the students a picture of the Grand Canyon. Ask if they have any ideas about what could cause such a great hole in the ground.

Explore

1. Students can use sand, dirt, and rocks to build a mountain on a cookie tray. Have them draw the mountain on a lab page.
2. Use a spray bottle to spray the mountain. Ask, What changes did you notice? Write what you saw on your lab page.
3. Pour water on the mountain, first gently, then harder. What changes did you notice? Record your findings
4. Rebuild your mountain. Decide what types of

things would help your mountain stay in place. (Craft sticks or plastic toys can represent trees, etc.) Add something to help your mountain.

5. Draw the new mountain with the "trees" in place.
6. Use the spray bottle to spray the mountain. What happened this time? Write your findings on your lab page.
7. Pour water on the mountain as before. What happened this time? Write on your lab page.

Develop

Sing the song to the tune of "She'll be Coming Round the Mountain."

Water wears down the mountains
when it comes.
Water wears down the mountains
when it comes.
Water wears down the mountains, water wears
down the mountains, water wears down the
mountains when it comes.

Water causes erosion all around,
Water causes erosion all around.
Water causes erosion,
Yes, it causes erosion,
Water causes erosion when it comes.

Have children write a sentence or two at the bottom of their lab pages to explain how water can affect the land.

Extend

Take students on a walk around the school grounds to look for signs of erosion. Check water drainage areas. Have the children explain what they see and why they think it happens.

71

As a result of activities in grades K-4, all students should develop understanding of personal health, characteristics and changes in populations, types of resources, changes in environments, and science and technology in local challenges.

Air Pollution

types of resources

- The supply of many resources is limited.

changes in environments

- Changes in environments can be natural or influenced by humans. Some changes are good, some are bad, and some are neither good nor bad. Pollution is a change in the environment that can influence the health, survival, or activities of organisms, including humans.

Also addresses earth science standards for understanding properties of earth materials.

Materials

- tally sheets (Engage)
- 4" x 4" cardboard squares, aluminum foil, tape, hole punch, string, petroleum jelly, craft sticks, magnifiers (Explore)

Engage

Students will tally cars on a sheet according to these categories:

One person in car
Two people in car
Three or more people in car

Ask students to meet you at the front of the school first thing in the morning, or take them there just at the end of the day when there is the most traffic. Time them for five minutes as they count the vehicles and the number of people in each. When you all return to the classroom, discuss their observations. Graph the data. Ask the students to discuss alternatives to driving alone.

Explore

Give students four-inch squares of cardboard to make pollution catchers. Ask them to cover the squares with foil and make it as smooth as possible. They can secure it with tape. Punch a hole at a corner and tie string through the hole to hang the catcher. Help children use a craft stick to spread a thin layer of petroleum jelly on both sides of the foil, being careful not to touch the petroleum jelly after putting it on the foil.

Decide where to hang the catchers. Think of some spots that may have more air pollution and some spots that may have less. Say, Record on your science lab page where you hang your catcher. Also write your prediction about which will collect the most pollution.

Check the catchers and bring them in after a day or two. Check for dirt. Have the children draw the results and make comparisons. Using magnifiers, try to determine what the dirt is and try to find out where it came from. Discuss your observations.

Develop

Create posters that encourage adults to drive in carpools as a way to help keep the air clean. Show your posters to family and friends.

Extend

Poll your family and friends to see if they drive alone or in carpools. Encourage them to find someone else to drive with to help with the unwanted exhaust and pollution in the air.

0-7424-2789-7 *Inexpensive Science Experiments for Young Children*

Ways to Clean Water

types of resources

- The supply of many resources is limited.

changes in environments

- Changes in environments can be natural or influenced by humans. Some changes are good, some are bad, and some are neither good nor bad. Pollution is a change in the environment that can influence the health, survival, or activities of organisms, including humans.

Also addresses earth science standards for understanding properties of earth materials; science and technology standards for abilities of technological design and understanding about science and technology.

Materials

- lab page (p. 79), buckets of clean water, dirt, trash, oil, clear plastic jars, coffee filters, cheesecloth, white fabric (Explore)

Engage

Ask students to brainstorm why water is important to us. What do we do with it, what do we need it for? Discuss their ideas.

Explore

Students can work in groups.

1. Students can work in groups. Give each group a large bucket of water. Tell students to look at the clean water. What does it look like? Does it smell? Write observations on a lab page.
2. Simulate pollutants in the water by adding, trash, dirt, oil, etc. Say, Make observations of the water again and write them on your lab page.

3. Ask the students how we can clean water. Do we use machines? Chemicals? Things from nature? Write their ideas on the board.

Groups can experiment with materials to use as water filters. They can use jars of the dirtied water. Let them choose from coffee filters, cheese cloth, white cotton fabric (such as T-shirt material), etc., and pour the dirty water through them into clean jars. They can also try letting the dirt settle out of the water and the trash float to the top. Have them record the steps they use to clean the water. Compare the different samples of water to see which method worked best.

Develop

Decide if your water is clean. Research in books or on the Internet the processes used to clean water. Did you include any steps in your experiments that did the same things?

Extend

Plan a field trip to a local water treatment plant or a water source. Have the students examine the water to see if they think it is clean.

0-7424-2789-7 *Inexpensive Science Experiments for Young Children*

More Ways to Clean Water

types of resources

• The supply of many resources is limited.

changes in environments

• Changes in environments can be natural or influenced by humans. Some changes are good, some are bad, and some are neither good nor bad. Pollution is a change in the environment that can influence the health, survival, or activities of organisms, including humans.

Also addresses earth science standards for understanding properties of earth materials; science and technology standards for abilities of technological design and understanding about science and technology.

 ## Materials

• glass of brown water (Engage)
• two-liter bottle cut in half for each group, cotton, gravel, pebbles, sand (Explore 1)
• large bowl, heavy drinking glass, plastic wrap or large plastic bag, (Develop) small stone (Explore 2)
• lab page, p. 79 (Develop)

Engage

Offer a child a glass of dirty brown water to drink. When the child refuses the water, ask her or him to explain why. Discuss with the class what is wrong with the water. Would it be healthy to drink? Would it taste all right?

Explore

1. Students create a water filter. Cut a soda bottle in half across the middle. Put the top half of the bottle upside down in the bottom half. Add cotton to the mouth of the bottle; stuff it in tightly. Put gravel on top of the

cotton, put pebbles on top of the gravel, and put sand on top of the pebbles. Test your water filter. Compare the water that goes through this system to the water you cleaned in the last activity (p. 73).

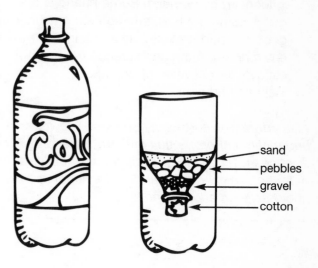

2. Students learn another way to clean water. Put some of the dirty water in a large bowl. Stand a clean, empty glass in the center of the bowl of water. Cover the bowl with plastic wrap secured by a rubber band but not pulled too tight. Put a stone in the center of the wrap above the glass. *(This creates a dip in the plastic for the water to drip into the glass.)* Set the bowl in the sun all day. Remove the stone and the plastic wrap. What is in the glass? *(Clean water)*

Develop

Have students draw one of the water cleaning systems on a science lab page. Identify and label the parts of the system and decide how the different parts helped clean the water.

Extend

Conduct further research to find out how water plants clean water for drinking and household use.

0-7424-2789-7 *Inexpensive Science Experiments for Young Children*

Food Chains

types of resources

- The supply of many resources is limited.

changes in environments

- Changes in environments can be natural or influenced by humans. Some changes are good, some are bad, and some are neither good nor bad. Pollution is a change in the environment that can influence the health, survival, or activities of organisms, including humans.

Also addresses life science standards for understanding organisms and environments.

Materials

- pieces of fabric or football flags, baseball base (Explore)

Engage

Teach students this song, to the tune (more or less) of "The Farmer in the Dell."

> The insects eat the plant,
> The insects eat the plant!
> Hi-ho, the food chain we know,
> The insects eat the plants.
>
> The fish eats the insects,
> The fish eats the insects!
> Hi-ho, the food chain we know,
> The fish eats the insects.
>
> The big fish eats the fish,
> The big fish eats the fish!
> Hi-ho, the food chain we know,
> The big fish eats the fish.
>
> The people eat the fish,
> The people eat the fish!
> Hi-ho, the food chain we know,
> The people eat the fish.

Explore

Play a game to show the food chain and how animals depend on each other to survive. Five people will be prey and the rest of the class will be predators. The students who are prey can have a piece of fabric tied loosely to a wrist or on a belt to identify them. The prey stand in the middle of the play area to begin. They can run around to avoid capture and touch home (use a baseball base for home), which represents a hiding place for them. But only one prey can be on home at a time. The predators are allowed six at a time into the play area to try to catch the prey. If the predators don't catch the prey, the predator dies and becomes the prey in the next round. The predators are allowed in the area for two minutes.

Each time a predator catches a prey, the predator reproduces—the prey becomes a predator. Record the number of predators and prey each round.

Develop

Explain what happens when there is not enough food for the prey in the game. Explain what happens when there is enough food for all the predators in the game.

Think of endangered species and relate this game to their survival and life.

Extend

Investigate other food chains. Create a chart that shows a food chain in action and how different plants and animals depend on each other.

0-7424-2789-7 *Inexpensive Science Experiments for Young Children*

Fighting Litter

types of resources

- The supply of many resources is limited.

changes in environments

- Changes in environments can be natural or influenced by humans. Some changes are good, some are bad, and some are neither good nor bad. Pollution is a change in the environment that can influence the health, survival, or activities of organisms, including humans.

Materials

- garden or household gloves, trash bags (Explore)

Engage

Say, We can all do something to make a difference in the world. I would like you to think of three things you can do to help make the world a better place. Brainstorm ideas together.

Explore

Have the class vote to adopt a park or the school grounds to keep litter-free. After they decide on the class adoption, students should then develop a plan of action to accomplish their goals.

Develop

Put the plan into action. Write letters to other classes about what your class is doing. Encourage them to help with your project or to develop a project of their own. Ask the teachers read the letters to their classes.

Extend

Make a class book to tell about how you can help to keep the earth clean. Include a report about your adoption project. Tell what you did.

We've got the whole world in our hands,
We've got the whole world in our hands.
We've got the whole world in our hands,
We've got the whole world in our hands.

We've got the land and the water in our hands.
We've got the plants and the animals in our hands.
We've got the whole world in our hands.

0-7424-2789-7 *Inexpensive Science Experiments for Young Children*

Question Investigation

Materials

- As students identify their questions, have them list materials they think they will need.
- My Inquiry page, p. 78 (Explore)

Engage

Create a science detective questions chart. Explain to students that they have been investigating science and now it is their turn to ask the questions.

Children can brainstorm all kinds of questions they have about plants, animals, their five senses, weather, etc.

Explore

Help students plan experiments to find out what they want to know. They can list materials they need. Have students use the inquiry form (p. 78) to tell how they did their investigations and what they found out.

Students should report their questions and investigations to their classmates.

Have groups of students replicate the investigations that other groups conducted to see if they get the same results.

Develop

Say, Think about your experiments and how you have become a science detective. Write a creative mystery and use the results of your science experiment to solve the mystery.

Have students tell their stories to the class.

Extend

Encourage students to conduct additional experiments to investigate interesting things in the world.

0-7424-2789-7 *Inexpensive Science Experiments for Young Children*

Name _____ Date _____

My Inquiry

Here is the question I have.

_____

This is how I can find out the answer.

_____

This is what we did. _____

This is what we found out. _____

Here is a picture to show our inquiry.

0-7424-2789-7 *Inexpensive Science Experiments for Young Children*

Name _____ Date _____

Science Lab Page

0-7424-2789-7 *Inexpensive Science Experiments for Young Children*

Science-Related Children's Literature

Senses/Human body

My Five Senses ....Aliki
Look Book ....Tana Hoban
What's What? A Guessing Game ....Mary Serfozo
What in the World? ....Eve Merriam
Sense Suspense: A Guessing Game for the Five Senses....Bruce McMillan
The Magic School Bus Inside the Human Body ....Joanna Cole
Berlioz the Bear ....Jan Brett

Weather

The Sun, the Wind and the Rain ....Lisa Westberg Peters
Gilberto and the Wind ....Marie Hall Ets
Feel the Wind ....Arthur Dorros
Air Is All Around You ....Franklyn M. Branley
The Wind Blew ....Pat Hutchins
The Mitten: A Ukrainian Folktale..........................Jan Brett
Cloudy with a Chance of Meatballs......................Judi Barrett

Environment

Bartholomew and the Oobleck.............................Dr. Seuss
Miss Rumphius ....Barbara Cooney
Nature Walk ....Douglas Florian
The Magic School Bus: At the Waterworks ....Joana Cole
Once There Was a Tree ....Natalia Romanova
Hungry Animals: My First Look at the Food Chain ....Pamela Hickman
Ten Seeds ....Ruth Brown
The Giving Tree...Shel Silverstein

Simple Machines/ Structures

On the Move..Brian Williams
How Do You Lift a Lion? ....Robert E. Wells
Tools ....Ann Morris
Mirette on the High Wire ....Emily Arnold McCully
Why Doesn't the Earth Fall Up? ....Vicki Cobb
The Three Little Pigs..Paul Galdone
The Three Billy Goats Gruff ....Paul Galdone
The Three Little Wolves and the Big Bad Pig ....Eugene Trivizas

Plants and Animals

From Seed to Plant ....Gail Gibbons
The Pumpkin Book ....Gail Gibbons
The Tiny Seed...Eric Carle
The Carrot Seed ....Ruth Krauss
Hello, Tree!...Joanne Ryder
On the Move: A Study of Animal Movement........................Joyce Pope
Animal Defenses: How Animals Protect Themselves..........Etta Kaner
Animals Eating: How Animals, Chomp, Chew,
    Slurp and Swallow ....Pamela Hickman
Birdsong ....Audrey Wood

Published by Instructional Fair. Copyright protected.

0-7424-2789-7 Inexpensive Science Experiments
for Young Children